Ferdinand Römer

The Bone Caves of Ojcow in Poland

Ferdinand Römer

The Bone Caves of Ojcow in Poland

ISBN/EAN: 9783337198350

Printed in Europe, USA, Canada, Australia, Japan

Cover: Foto ©Andreas Hilbeck / pixelio.de

More available books at **www.hansebooks.com**

THE
BONE CAVES OF OJCOW

LONDON PRINTED BY
SPOTTISWOODE AND CO., NEW-STREET SQUARE
AND PARLIAMENT STREET

SKULL OF URSUS SPELÆUS.

FROM A CAVE NEAR OJCOW IN RUSSIAN POLAND.

THE
BONE CAVES OF OJCOW
IN POLAND

BY

PROFESSOR DR FERD. RÖMER

TRANSLATED BY

JOHN EDWARD LEE, F.G.S., F.S.A.

AUTHOR OF 'ISCA SILURUM' ETC.
TRANSLATOR OF KELLER'S 'LAKE DWELLINGS,' MERK'S 'KESSLERLOCH' ETC.

LONDON
LONGMANS, GREEN, AND CO.
1884

All rights reserved

TRANSLATOR'S PREFACE.

A TRANSLATOR'S PREFACE consists, or at least ought to consist, of very few words. The mere fact of translation shows his opinion of the value of the memoir. Believing, as he does, that the subject is a very instructive one to many Englishmen who do not read German, he has done his best to make this interesting account generally available.

As the foreign measures are now very often used in English scientific works, they have not been reduced to their English equivalents, but a table is here given by which, with a trifling amount of trouble, any foreign measure mentioned may be reduced into English.

VILLA SYRACUSA, TORQUAY :[1] *October 1883.*

TABLE FOR CONVERTING FOREIGN MEASURES OF LENGTH INTO ENGLISH INCHES AND DECIMALS.

			English inches				English inches
1 millimetre		=	0·03937	5 centimetres		=	1·96854
2	,,	=	0·07874	6	,,	=	2·36226
3	,,	=	0·11811	7	,,	=	2·755
4	,,	=	0·15748	8	,,	=	3·14968
5	,,	=	0·19685	9	,,	=	3·54539
6	,,	=	0·23622	10 ,, or 1 decimetre		=	3·9371
7	,,	=	0·27559				
8	,,	=	0·31496	1 metre		=	39·37079
9	,,	=	0·35433	5	,,	=	196·85395
10 ,, or 1 centimetre		=	0·39371	10	,,	=	393·7079
				20	,,	=	787·4158
2	,,	=	0·78742	50	,,	=	1968·5395
3	,,	=	1·18113	100	,,	=	3937·079
4	,,	=	1·57484	1 kilometre		=	1093·633 Eng. yds.

[1] I may perhaps be allowed to add that Professor Römer, when lately in England, has kindly looked over most of this translation, and made a few trifling alterations. This is mentioned to give greater confidence in the accuracy of the translation. I think it right also to mention that I have received great assistance in the translation from Professor Boyd Dawkins, Dr. E. B. Tylor, Mr. W. S. Dallas, F.L.S., Dr. Gunther, F.R.S., and Dr. Chance, as well as from several medical friends here.

AUTHOR'S PREFACE.

THE CAVES now about to be described have for a length of time been partially known to the inhabitants of the district, but they first attracted general attention some years since, when the bottoms of the caves were worked for manure, the bed of earth being rich in bones, and containing a large quantity of phosphoric acid. The Cave of Jerzmanowice more especially has yielded these results since the year 1872. The author obtained his first information respecting these works from the mining officials of Upper Silesia, who had to visit professionally these places in Poland, and at the same time he received from this cave some single bones and teeth of the cave bear, and also some prehistoric flint implements. In the year 1874 a visit was made to the Cave of Jerzmanowice, and p oof was obtained that it contained a great quantity of bones of extinct animals, and also of implements of the ancient inhabitants.

This led to the determination of undertaking a thorough investigation of these caves, and of doing this if possible before the caves were cleared of their deposits for agricultural purposes, by which all the scientific data would be utterly lost.

On the application of the author, the necessary funds were granted by the Royal Prussian Ministry of Instruction. Thus in the spring of 1878 the work began, and was continued all through the summer. Several thousand specimens rewarded this labour. But the whole excavation could not be made in this first summer, more especially as during the excavation of this cave many other promising caves were discovered, and it appeared highly desirable that the investigation should be continued in the course of the following summer, 1879. And this time our grateful acknowledgments are due to the Royal Academy of Sciences at Berlin, who granted a considerable subsidy, which enabled the author to continue and complete his labours. In the course of the last summer several caves were entirely excavated, and not only so, but new ones were taken in hand.

With respect to the general results of the investigation, the specimens in the caves near Ojcow (pronounced Oĭzoff) agree on the whole with those of other well-known bone caves, and more especially resemble those of the caves of Moravia, although in some few instances there were peculiarities. In any case it was of interest to examine these caves, which are the most easterly of any European caves north of the Carpathians, so as to be able to compare them more especially with other German caves.

It is most certainly to be regretted, with respect to the specimens found in the caves of Ojcow, that it cannot be always positively stated from which bed in the caves they were taken, but the case is the same with most of the caves which have been excavated in Germany. This difficulty could only have been avoided, to a certain extent, if the work had gone on quite slowly and with great precaution, under the continued superintendence of the scientific manager of the excavation. Mr. O. Grube, who was entrusted by the author with the management of the work, has, however, done his best to indicate the position of all the specimens.

The whole of the objects obtained by the excavation, whether of fossil bones or prehistoric implements, have been deposited by the author in the Mineralogical Museum of the University of Breslau. The long delay in publishing this memoir has been caused by several circumstances beyond the control of the author.

FERD. ROEMER.

BRESLAU: *February* 1883.

NOTE BY THE TRANSLATOR.

As some of the terms used by Professor Virchow in his description of the skulls from Ojcow (page 30) may be new to some readers of the ensuing paper, it has been thought advisable to copy, with the leave of Professor Boyd Dawkins, a page from his late work (page 190), entitled 'Cave Hunting' (Macmillan, 1874):

'The term cephalic index indicates the ratio of the extreme transverse to the extreme longitudinal diameter of the skull, the latter measurement being taken as unity (Huxley).

'The most convenient classification of crania is that adopted by Dr. Thurnham and Professor Huxley,[1] and based on the cephalic index.

I. Dolicho-cephali, or long skulls, with cephalic index	at or below 73
Subdolicho-cephali	from 70 to 73
II. Ortho-cephali or oval skulls	,, 74 ,, 79
Sub-brachy-cephali	,, 77 ,, 79
III. Brachy-cephali or broad skulls	at or above 80

'It has been objected that skull form is of no value in determining race, because it varies so much at the present time among the same peoples, presenting the extremes of dolicho- and brachy-cephalism, as well as every kind of asymmetry. This, however, is due to our very abnormal conditions of life, and to the mixture of different races, brought about by the needs of commerce, as in Manchester and Vienna, as is pointed out by Mr. Bradley ("Mem. Lit. and Phil. Soc." Manchester, vol. v. p. 213). In prehistoric times, neither of these causes of variation made themselves seriously felt. There was little if any peaceful movement of races, but war was the normal condition, and society was not sufficiently advanced to remove man from the influence of his natural environment. The objection may therefore be dismissed as not applicable to the skulls in question.'

Professor Virchow, in his notice of the Ojcow skulls (page 30), seems to have taken 100 millimetres as 'unity.'

[1] *Anthropological Memoirs*, vols. i. and iii., Huxley and Laing, 'Prehistoric Remains in Caithness.'

CONTENTS.

	PAGE
TRANSLATOR'S PREFACE. TABLE OF ENGLISH AND FOREIGN MEASURES	v
AUTHOR'S PREFACE	vii
NOTE BY TRANSLATOR	ix

I. GEOLOGICAL AND TOPOGRAPHICAL SITUATION OF THE CAVES, AND GENERAL ACCOUNT OF THEM. MODE OF OCCURRENCE OF THE ANIMAL AND HUMAN BONES IN THE CAVES . . . 2

II. NOTICES OF EACH OF THE CAVES :
  1. THE CAVE OF JERZMANOWICE . 4
  2. THE CAVE OF KOZARNIA . 9
  3. THE LOWER CAVE OF WIERSZCHOW . 10
  4. THE UPPER CAVE OF WIERSZCHOW . 14
  5. THE CAVE OF ZDÓJECKA . 15
  6. THE CAVES OF CZAJOWICE . 15
  7. THE CAVE OF SADLANA . 16
  8. THE CAVES OF BEMBEL . 16
  9. THE CAVE OF GÓRENICE . 17

III. LIST OF THE SKULLS AND BONES OF THE EXTINCT ANIMALS, AND OF THE HUMAN REMAINS AND IMPLEMENTS . . 18
  A. ANIMALS 18
  B. HUMAN REMAINS AND IMPLEMENTS . 28
    I. SKULLS AND BONES . . . 28
    II. IMPLEMENTS 36
      a. MADE FROM STONE AND GLASS . 36
      b. SPECIMENS MADE FROM BONE . 37
        1. Tools . . . 37
        2. Objects for ornament, amulets, or games . 38
      c. OBJECTS MADE OF BURNT CLAY . . 39
      d. OBJECTS MADE OF BRONZE, SILVER, AND IRON . 39

IV. GENERAL RESULTS . 40

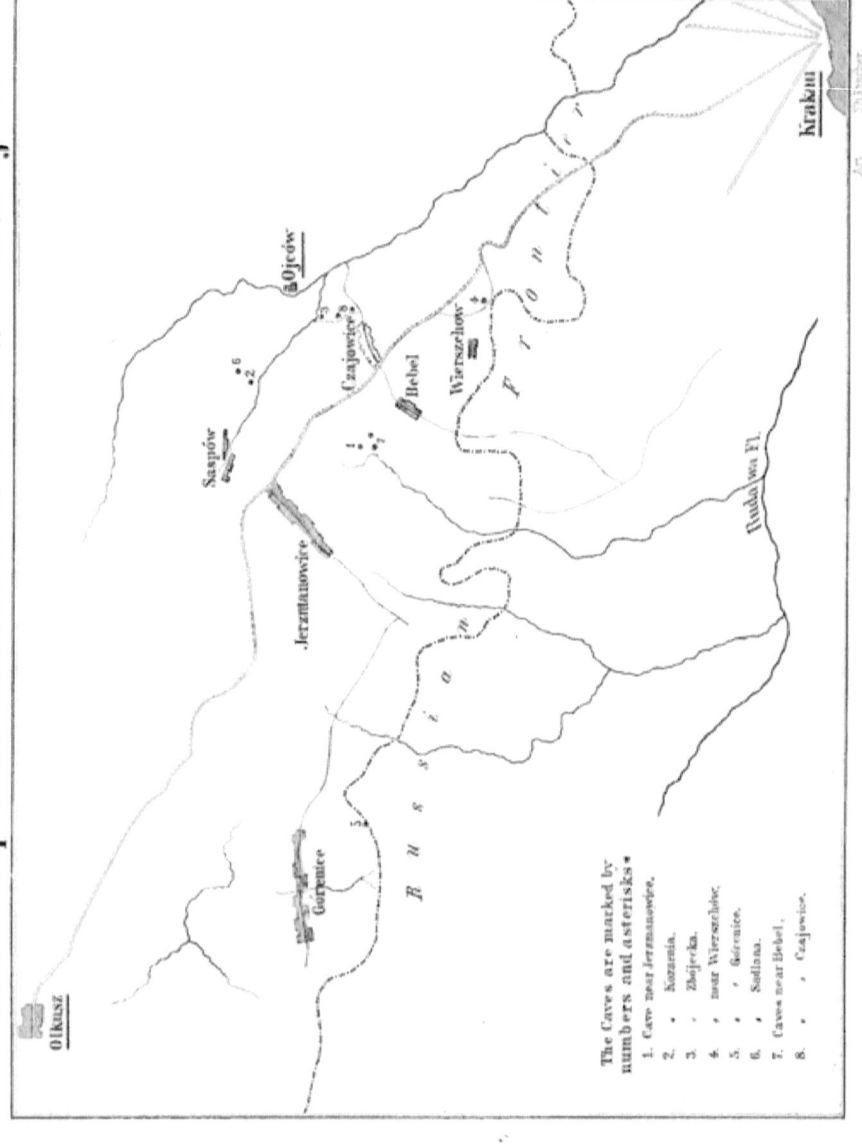

THE
BONE CAVES OF OJCOW.

The Caves now under consideration occur in the southern division of the range of hills belonging to the different members of the oolitic formation; this range of hills runs nearly continuously from Cracow to Czenstochau, a distance of about fifteen (German) miles, and forms a striking character in relation to the orography and geology of Western Poland.

In the immediate neighbourhood of Cracow indeed this range of hills will hardly be noticed; the white oolitic limestone is only seen in single rocky heights, more especially the hill near Podgorze and the more considerable rise out of the plain of the Vistula, on which is situated the monastery of Bielany. Again, for a (German) mile north of Cracow, as far as the Russian frontier, there is a thick covering of loess, which hides the underlying rock from view: but as soon as the frontier is passed the character of the district changes. The underlying rock comes to light everywhere, more especially in the denuded narrow valleys which run in a southerly direction, where they spread out into the valley of the Vistula. In these valleys, the sides of which are as precipitous as a wall, the jurassic beds may be seen, and even in some few cases occur as isolated prismatic rocks. The clear rapid brooks at the bottom of these valleys would almost lead one to imagine the existence of luxuriant meadows and lofty forests; in fact of lovely rural scenery, quite contrary to the prevailing uniformity and table-land of the Polish district, so that it has been jocosely termed the Polish Switzerland. The valley of Ojcow and the adjacent valleys exhibit this peculiarity more especially.

Such is the nature of the country in which the Caves occur which are now about to be described.

GEOLOGICAL AND TOPOGRAPHICAL SITUATION AND GENERAL REMARKS AS TO THE CAVES.

The caves all occur in the white limestone of the oolitic formation—the prevailing rock of the district. It consists of a series of strata in all many hundred feet thick, which is so indistinctly divided into separate beds that it has usually been considered uniformly massive. It is a compact white oolitic limestone with a splintery or flatly conchoidal fracture, and very often forms precipitous cliffs.[1]

In all these caves, the entrances vary from ten to thirty feet above the level of the valley. Probably they were originally at the same level as the valley itself, but from its erosion they appear to have become higher. In some cases, the entrance is narrow and as it were in a fissure; sometimes it is wide and arched over. From the entrance the caves penetrate more or less deeply into the rock; in some cases they become wider, and then again end in fissures. The floor in general is uneven; occasionally it sinks suddenly, and then again rises. The character of these caves is exactly like that of other caves in limestone rocks, and they more particularly resemble those of the Franconian oolite in the district of Streitberg and Muggendorf; in fact, the general appearance of the country there reminds one of the country round Ojcow.

The solid rock is very seldom seen on the floor of the caves. As a general rule, there is a deposit more or less thick of broken stones and earth. The pieces of stone are angular fragments from an inch in diameter to the size of the fist, and consist of white jurassic rock, similar to that forming the sides of the cavern. Amongst them are a few larger blocks of limestone, varying from the size of a man's head up to several cubic feet. The earth fills the intervals between these angular stones; it very seldom forms a distinct bed of itself. It is of a dark brown colour, and when carefully examined seems to be a calcareous clay consisting of extremely fine particles; when moist, it is plastic and very adhesive. This mixture of limestone fragments and brown earth forms the deposit more or less considerable, but sometimes six or eight feet thick on the bottom of all the caves. If we ask how this deposit was formed, it may be replied almost undoubtedly that the pieces of limestone, thus heaped up, gradually crumbled from the top and sides of the cavern. The limestone, although firm and compact when fresh, is permeated by numerous fine cracks or fissures which when weathered are more

---

[1] It contains numerous organic remains, more especially the *Rhynchonella trilobata*, which is the characteristic species. Hence it has been called the bed of '*Rhynchonella trilobata*,' or 'Obere Felsenkalk.' See F. Roemer's *Geology of Upper Silesia*, pp. 259–61.

distinctly seen, and in course of time cause the rock to fall to pieces in angular fragments. On isolated walls of rock this disintegration of the stone may be distinctly seen, as small pieces become loose and fall down. People who have remained some time in the caves have occasionally heard small pieces fall from the roof. In no single case had the stones forming the floor of the cave been subjected to the action of water. This theory cannot be maintained for a moment, as may be shown both from the angularity of form and from the similarity of the rock. Rounded pebbles, such as are found in the brooks flowing in the valleys beneath, are never found in the caves: there are no pieces of any other rock except the limestone forming the sides of the cavern.

There is a little more difficulty in deciding positively the origin of the brown earth. The idea of its having been washed in from the outside is probably not worth considering; the more probable explanation is that it is the argillaceous residuum of the limestone which has been acted upon by the carbonic acid contained in the water. Some small amount of clay is, in fact, a peculiarity of the limestone.

In most of the caves there are horizontal layers of coarsely crystalline stalagmite on the floor; they are usually only some inches thick, but in some cases the thickness is more than a foot. Numerous root-like stalactites hang down from the roof, but none have been noticed of any peculiar size or beauty. In most of the caves the formation of stalactites and of stalagmites on the floor still continues, as water containing lime is continually dropping from the roof.

MODE IN WHICH THE ANIMAL AND HUMAN BONES OCCUR IN THE CAVES.

In all the caves yet examined in this district both animal and human bones have been found in large or small quantities. They occur in rubbish at the bottom of the caves at various depths; sometimes they are under a covering of stalagmite, and not unfrequently they are embedded in it. Most of the bones are completely changed chemically, so that everything which is gelatinous and soluble in water has disappeared, and only the lime of the texture remains. Even this is so porous that, for instance, if water be poured through the broken end of a thigh bone of the cave bear, it will immediately run out through any chance opening at the other end.

The bones and skulls occur separately, and skeletons are never found entire. Thus, in excavating, bones and teeth of several hundred individuals of the cave bear were discovered, but in no one instance was there a complete skeleton; there was not even a single case of the lower jaws being united with any of the numerous skulls of this animal. Even the two halves of the under jaws were almost always separated; they were only united in one single instance.

The bones and skulls lying in the damp parts of the ground were quite soft and fragile, and great care was required to secure them uninjured. But after exposure to the air they became so solid as to require no further attention. Only the teeth, and more especially the canines of the cave bear, cracked and flew in pieces on being dried in the air; they had either to be soaked in lime water, or dried gradually with the greatest care.

NOTICES AND DESCRIPTION OF ALL THE CAVES WHICH HAVE BEEN INVESTIGATED.

Numerous caves are known to exist in this district; and many more would doubtless be found if well looked for. As yet only some of those first discovered, and such as yielded good results from their contents, have been examined. These will be described in the following pages, and their contents duly noted.[1]

1. The Cave of Jerzmanowice (*in German 'Fledermausgrotto'*).

This cave lies to the south-east of the village of Jerzmanowice (provincially known as Wierzbanowice) not far from the road leading from Olkusz to Cracow; it is on the left slope of a small valley dry at the bottom (see the sketch map). The entrance, which is three metres forty centimetres high, opens to the south, and is about thirty metres above the level of the valley: it is in a nearly precipitous cliff, about fifteen metres high.

A little above the entrance there is a peculiar hole about one square metre in size, of a regularly quadrangular shape, evidently artificial, but intended for some purpose not yet explained. The house of F. Ferdek, the proprietor of the cave, stands near the entrance.

The cavern from the entrance runs back about 230 metres, and winds about considerably, but on the whole it takes an east and west direction into the mountain. It follows the course of the ridge, which is tolerably flat and overgrown with brushwood; it slopes decidedly more to the west than to the east. The whole cavern is made up of a series of several grottoes or caves, connected by narrow passages. One of these grottoes is almost regularly arched and dome-shaped, and is about thirty feet in height. The floor is decidedly uneven, but on the whole may be said to be horizontal. When excavated, the first bed generally is one of

---

[1] The notice of these caves is given according to their size, and the importance of the results obtained from them, not according to their geographical position.

angular pieces of limestone, the space between which is filled with dark brown earth, feeling moist and unctuous from the water which percolates it. Some larger pieces of rock are found amongst this rubbish, in some cases several cubic feet in size.

This bed of stony rubbish is often several metres thick, and beneath it in general there is a bed of solid crystalline stalagmite from ten to twenty centimetres thick. Below this there is again a bed of pieces of rock mixed with earth, which here is less moist than that above the stalagmite. In the very lowest bed the pieces of stone are fewer in number, and the earth is quite dry and powdery. The original rock was never reached, although in some places the excavation was continued to a depth of nine metres.

This cave of Jerzmanowice is the largest and most extensive cavern in the district, and it is also the richest in the remains of extinct animals and of prehistoric human implements. Fossil mammalian remains were found everywhere, both in the upper and in the lower beds forming the floor. The bones and skulls of the larger animals occurred more especially near the sides of each of the chambers. The rich deposit of bones found in this cave first became known by the partial excavation of the floor in 1872 and in subsequent years, the floor having then been excavated to procure the brown earth, which was valuable as manure, on account of its containing phosphates. Since then systematic excavations have been made in different parts of the cave under the direction of the author, so that probably on the whole about a third of the floor has been examined. The excavation of the cave earth has been given up since the above-named year, as the result did not pay for the labour.

The following species of animals were noted:

1. *Ursus spelæus* (the Cave Bear).—The remains of this animal were by far the most abundant. Bones, skulls, and single teeth occur in all parts of the cave in great abundance, and in fact both in the upper and the lower beds; they were most plentiful in the lower beds, at a depth of five metres. No perfect skeleton was ever found, but only single bones and skulls. The number of individual animals buried in the deposits of the cave is extraordinary, and may be reckoned by thousands. Although only a very small portion of the floor of the cave was excavated by us, yet the bears' canines collected by us formed a heap a foot high. Besides this, a very large number of teeth of this description must have been found and given away in the country by the labourers when digging the brown earth for manure; the regular form and the shining smooth crown of the tooth must have attracted their attention. My belief is that we should not be far wrong in estimating the whole number of canines of the cave bear found in the cavern as at least 4,000, so that as each animal had four canines, this would make the number of individual bears 1,000. But as only about a third of the floor of the cave has been hitherto excavated, the whole number of animals ought to be reckoned much higher. We cannot of course imagine that so large a number of these animals lived at the same time in the cave, or even in the surrounding district; but there was doubtless a period of extraordinary length

during which a long series of many **succeeding generations of these animals lived in the cave**, and, when they died, their remains **were covered by the débris of the rock.** If we could **venture to** imagine that, like recent bears, only one family could live at the same time in the **cave,** and that the lifetime of the cave bear was of the same duration as that of **the brown** bear, to which it is so nearly allied, we should have some kind of data on which to **found the** length of the period when the cave was inhabited by bears.

Besides the bones and skulls of full-grown animals, there were also the remains of **younger** ones of all ages; we may especially mention the under jaws of sucking animals, only 78 millimetres in length, in which the teeth still remaining in the jaw have not yet protruded.

The remains of other mammalia are very few compared with those of the cave bear.

2. *Hyæna spelæa* (Cave Hyæna).—The halves of two under jaws nearly perfect, belonging to different animals, and a few loose molars.

3. *Felis spelæa* (Cave Lion).—The halves of two under jaws, belonging to two animals, and a humerus.

4. *Felis lynx* (Lynx).—A left under jaw.

5. *Canis lupus* var.—The halves of several under jaws, nearly perfect.

6. *Canis sp.* (a passage between the Wolf and the Fox).—The halves of several under jaws.

7. *Canis vulpes* (Fox).—Several skulls, and numerous halves of the under jaw.

8. *Meles taxus* (Badger).—Several skulls.

9. *Fœtorius putorius* (Polecat).—An under jaw.

10. *Elephas primigenius* (Mammoth).—The molar of an animal nearly full grown was found in the more distant part of the cavern, about 228 metres from the entrance, at a depth of several feet. Naturally it is not to be imagined that this **animal, when alive, had found its way** through all the winding passages of the cave, so that this tooth must have been brought there.

11. *Plecotus auritus* (Long-eared Bat).—Numerous skulls.

12. *Vesperugo pipistrellus* (Dwarf Bat).—Numerous skulls.

13. *Vesperugo serotinus* (Late-flying Bat).—Two skulls.

14. *Vespertilio murinus* (Common Bat).—Numerous skulls **and bones.**

15. *Talpa europæa* (Mole).—Several under jaws.

The numerous remains proving the existence of human inhabitants of the cave in very far distant ages, consist partly of the bones of the human skeleton, and partly of implements and other traces of human industry. The bones are not of any peculiar interest, as they **present** no marked difference from those of the present inhabitants of the district. No perfect skull has yet been found. Greater interest attaches to the implements; they are made either of **stone or bone.** The most common are what are called flint knives, viz. flint flakes the length of a finger, and from half an inch to two inches in breadth, cutting on both sides at a very acute angle. Most of them are flat flakes, the cutting sides of which are nearly parallel (see Plate I. Figs. 3, 4, and 5), as if they had been struck off by a single blow from a larger flint core or nucleus without any further labour having been bestowed upon them.[1] The double-edged knives of an oval or lancet-shape are less numerous; they were apparently made into their peculiar form by repeated small blows from another hard substance, so that additional care was required in their manipulation (see Plate I. Figs. 7 and 9). One specimen also was found rather flattened in form, one end of which had regular teeth; it evidently had been used as a saw (see Plate I. Fig. 2); it probably had been manipulated in the same manner. On the other hand, no polished flint tools were found. The flint implements all belong to the older stone age. It is also remarkable that in this cave, as in most of the others near Ojcow, no stone celts have been found.

The flint of which these implements are made appears exactly like that of the chalk formation of Northern Europe, and which is found spread over the whole northern plain of Germany in the form of diluvial gravel. But, in fact, it is quite different, as it comes from the upper jurassic limestone beds in the neighbourhood. Certain beds of this formation are in fact quite filled with nodules of flint,[2] and whole heaps of them may be seen lying on the road from Olkusz to Ojcow, so that the original cave-dwellers were not in want of material to work up. In fact, in this respect, they were more favoured than any of the ancient inhabitants living further northwards, there being no chalk till we arrive at the island of Rügen or the Danish islands. Implements of other kinds of stone were also found in the cave, among which may be especially mentioned a rounded cuboidal piece of northern diorite, about the size of the fist (see Plate V. Fig. 11). This stone occurs almost everywhere in the northern

---

[1] This probably must be taken with a little reservation. No doubt these flakes were struck off at a single blow from the cores, but in order to obtain the peculiar shape or section as drawn (Plate I. Figs. 3, 4, and 5), the flint nucleus or 'core' must have been as it were previously prepared. The annexed woodcut, copied from a sketch given to me by my friend Dr. H. Woodward, will explain this more clearly. The outer flakes would be what are called 'wasters.' It appears to me somewhat similar to the drawing of the 'core' given in Dr. Evans' *Ancient Stone Implements*, p. 18.—TR.

[2] See F. Roemer's *Geology of Upper Silesia*, pp. 200, 202.

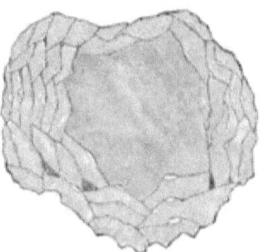

plain in the shape of gravel, and it is found also on the rises between Olkusz and Ojcow. Several pieces of stone were also found, which apparently had been used as grinding or polishing stones (see Plate V. Figs. 8–10). The material is sandy argillaceous rock, such as does not occur in the immediate neighbourhood of the cave, but at some little distance in the district of Krzeszowice.

Numerous bone implements were found here; some were evidently to be used as tools, others again were only used as ornaments. To the first class belong numerous pieces of bone of different shapes, all sharpened at one end, which had probably been used as borers (see Plates II. and III.). Some of them are perforated at the other end, as if they had been worn on a string or thong (see Plate II. Fig. 3). A unique specimen of a curved knife was also found; it was made out of a wild boar's tusk, one half of which had been ground away, so that the bent cutting edge is formed of the outer coat of the enamel of the tusk (see Plate IV. Fig. 8). Amongst the ornaments may be mentioned a wild boar's tusk, perforated at both ends (see Plate IV. Fig. 2), which probably had been used as a neck ornament; also some rather angular bone beads, which evidently had been intended to be threaded on a string.

Numerous pieces of burnt pottery gave further evidence of the existence of man in the cave. They are all of very rough manufacture, unglazed, and with large pieces of quartz mixed up with the clay; they are so imperfectly burnt, that on the inside the colour is still black or dark grey, and there are few cases in which the red colour goes quite through. Some of the pottery, from being so imperfectly burnt, is very porous, and cannot have been used for boiling fluids, but only for keeping dry materials, such as corn, berries, &c. The traces of hearths or fireplaces used by man can also be proved by the charcoal, pottery, and animals' bones, which decidedly characterise these places. In one locality, six metres from the entrance of the cave, two distinct beds could be seen marked by charcoal and burnt bones; they lay one above the other, but were separated by a thick mass of deposit. Immediately under a bed of stalagmite, some centimetres thick, there was a deposit of moist, blue-green, argillaceous matter, thirty centimetres thick, and immediately beneath this the upper fire-hearth. It was distinguished not only by the charcoal, but by bones, more especially those of the boar, the ox, the reindeer, the cave bear, and of several kinds of birds. The bones had been partly artificially broken, and blackened by the action of fire. The thickness of this hearth varied from eight to ten centimetres. Beneath it was a loamy bed, half a metre thick, containing flint flakes, pottery, split bones, but with few pieces of limestone. Beneath this bed was the second hearth, with charcoal, fifteen centimetres in thickness. This lower hearth lay on a deposit of large angular pieces of limestone and moist unctuous earth. The beds with charcoal extended probably two and a half square metres in all.

From the foregoing facts it may be considered certain that the cave was for a long course of years inhabited by men of a very low grade of civilisation, contemporary with the cave bear and the reindeer. Most certainly the intermediate bed between the two charcoal layers, and which was formed slowly, must indicate the period when the cave was inhabited. With respect to the co-existence of man and the cave bear, a very important fact is that a piece of rock a foot long, taken out of a bed of solid crystalline stalagmite lying several feet deep, contained a vertebra of the cave bear firmly embedded, and also an undoubted flint implement made by human hands. It may be further mentioned that at a short distance from this great cavern, in the direction of the 'strike' of the mountain, there is a small 'fissure-like' cave, in which numerous large bones of the mammoth (*Elephas primigenius*) are reported to have been found.

2. THE CAVE OF KOZARNIA (*in German* 'Ziegenstall').

This cave is in the district of the village of Saspow, which belongs to the Lordship of Pieskowa Skala. It lies in a small grass valley running north and south, which somewhat further on joins the larger valley running east and west; this afterwards leads into the valley of Ojcow. The nearest house is that of the forester, some hundred paces distant. The entrance to the cave opens to the west, and is on the left side of the valley, about ten metres high above the level. The valley is usually dry. The entrance is like a great wide-open door, and the cave inside runs back fifty-nine metres into the mountain; it is arched over and nearly straight, so that it is lighted almost throughout by the daylight from the entrance; there is only one short and nearly tubular offset, which gradually diminishes in size and runs from this arched main portion of the cave near the end towards the north. The entrance is now seven metres broad and three metres and a third high; originally it was by no means so large, but it has increased in size. The cave was excavated in the year 1877, for the sake of procuring the manure earth, and so the entrance was made wider.

The deposits on the floor of the cave were from two to four metres deep, and consisted of angular pieces of stone mixed with brown earth; the latter was separated from the stones by sieves, and then used as manure.

This cave proved to be very rich in the remains of extinct animals, and also of human implements. Unfortunately only a small portion of these have been preserved and secured for scientific examination.

The excavation had for the most part been made by the Administration of the Lordship of Pieskowa Skala, before the author first heard of the existence of the cave, and then only the deposits in the further part of the cavern were untouched. Some few bones of the larger animals which had been found in the excavation were subsequently secured. By far the larger portion had been carried away and were lost for ever.

The bones and skulls of the following animals were noticed:

1. *Ursus spelæus.*—Teeth, vertebræ, and other bones. On the whole, however, the remains of this species were less abundant than in the cave of Jerzmanowice.

2. *Hyæna spelæa.*—Two molars of the under jaw.

3. *Canis lupus.*—Several imperfect under jaws.

4. *Canis lagopus.*—The halves of several under jaws.

5. *Elephas primigenius.*—Two well-preserved molars of young animals, and fragments of tusks.

6. *Rhinoceros tichorhinus.*—A portion of the left upper jaw with the two last molars.

7. *Sus scrofa.*—Numerous teeth and fragments of skulls.

8. *Cervus tarandus.*—Numerous pieces of antlers—a few of very large size. Most of them may be considered as 'cast' antlers, from the good state of preservation of the lower end. Some of them are still fixed in portions of the skull.

9. *Bos primigenius.*—One well-preserved half under jaw.

10. *Equus fossilis.*—Bones of the extremities and teeth.

There were also bones and teeth of numerous recent mammalia, both large and small, especially of the stag, roe, sheep, wild cat, marten, fox, badger, &c.

Prehistoric human implements were also found in this cave in great numbers, more especially flint knives, grinding-stones of black slate, borers of bone, one of which was perforated at the end, and last, but not least, a tusk of *Ursus spelæus* which had been worn on a string, and which is of peculiar interest as it shows the contemporaneous existence of man and the cave bear. Another singular specimen is a needle with an 'eye,' made out of hard bone (see Plate IV. Fig. 10). Besides these, there were vessels of burnt clay of very rough manufacture, a spindle-whorl, also of burnt clay, and numerous bones of the extremities of mammalia, which had been split artificially, and, as far as could be ascertained, partly roasted in the fire.

3. THE LOWER CAVE OF WIERSZCHOW (*Mammoth Cave*).

This cave lies south of Ojcow, near the village of Wierszchow, close to the Russian-Austrian frontier, on the left slope of a small valley which is dry in summer (see the Sketch Map). The entrance of the cave, which can only be reached by climbing up a steep incline, is sixteen metres above the level of the valley. It is high and broad. An isolated rock stands in front of it looking like a gateway.

The inside of the cave is formed by a simple arch thirteen metres wide and nineteen metres in length. There are only two side ramifications, and these are at the further end. That on the left is nearly two metres high and three metres and a quarter broad, and it extends for fourteen metres, but gradually diminishes in size. That on the right is only six metres long, and one metre high and the same in breadth. The floor was just like that of the other caves, and consisted of a deposit several metres thick of angular pieces of limestone and brown argillaceous earth.

For a series of years, viz. from 1873 to 1879, this cave had been worked for the sake of anthropology and archæology by Count Johann Zawisza of Warsaw, so that its contents are more certainly known than those of the other caves. In the year 1878 I had the opportunity of seeing, when visiting the place, that the examination of the cave was carried on by the Count with the greatest care. What was, in fact, of more especial consequence, he had carefully noted the exact situation in the different beds of the floor where each of the specimens was found. In the other caves the excavation could only be carried on by artificial lighting, but in this cave daylight was available for the whole of the work. From the height of the entrance the outer light could reach all the front part of the cave, and this proved so favourable that even the smallest objects could not easily be passed over. Count Zawisza has already published the results of his excavations in several papers.[1] In these reports he has called the cave in question the 'Mammoth Cave,' on account of the great number of teeth and bones of *Elephas primigenius* found in it. The floor of the cave was, in fact, as rich in animal remains as in prehistoric human implements and bones.

Count Zawisza has mentioned the following animals which have been determined by Dr. O. Fraas of Stuttgart, and Dr. A. Slosarski of Warsaw:

1. *Ursus spelæus.*—This was the most abundant species in the cave, as well as in those already described; its remains were especially numerous in the lowest bed of the floor; bones and teeth were very abundant, but human remains were not found by Count Zawisza so low in the deposit.

2. *Ursus arctos.*—The remains of one animal.

3. *Canis lupus.*

4. *Canis lagopus.*—Not rare, in fact numerous under jaws were found.

5. *Canis vulpes.*

6. *Meles taxus.*

7. *Rhinoceros tichorhinus* or *antiquitatis.*—Three molars and several single bones.

8. *Elephas primigenius.*—The bones and teeth of at least three animals were found, besides which numerous implements, made artificially out of ivory, led to the conclusion that this animal must have been plentiful. Most of the bones were found in the left offset of the cavern, under a bed about half a foot thick of unctuous clay, together with bones of

---

[1] 1. *Poszukiwania Archeologiczne w Polsce,* opisał Jan Zawisza; *Recherches Archéologiques en Pologne.* Warszawa, 1874 (35 S. and 21 Taf.). 2. *Dalsze Poszukiwania Archeologiczne w Polsce,* opisał Jan Zawisza; *Suite des recherches Archéologiques en Pologne,* par Jean Zawisza. Warszawa, 1876 (8°. 26 S. and 6 Taf.). 3. *La caverne du Mammouth en Pologne,* par M. le Comte Zawisza, Planches XII., XIII., XIV. *Mémoires de la Soc. d'Anthropol.* t. 1, 2 Série, Paris, 1878, pp. 430–447. 4. *Poszukiwania Archeologiczne w Polsce,* 1877, 1878, and 1879; *Rech. Archéol. en Pologne,* par Jean Zawisza, 1878, and 1879. Warszawa, 1879 (30 S. and 3 Taf.). 5. *Wiadomości Archeologiczne IV.* Warszawa, 1882, pp. 1–18; *Résumé Français,* l.c. pp. 21–30, t. 1, 3.

other animals, more especially the antlers of the reindeer and the elk; they were also associated with numerous large and small flint implements. Amongst the bones found here may be especially mentioned a large tusk, a pelvis, and a great humerus. The fact that in the year 1878 five contiguous vertebræ belonging to the same animal were found lying together, indicates that it was not merely that single bones of this animal had been brought into the cave by rapacious animals or by man, but that the whole body had been brought into the cave and buried there.

9. *Cervus tarandus.*—Numerous bones and antlers of animals of all ages, from one year old up to those of great age.

10. *Cervus alces* (Elk).—Bones and antlers in abundance.

11. *Cervus elaphus.*—Rare.

12. *Cervus capreolus.*—Rare.

13. *Equus caballus fossilis.*—Numerous remains.

14. *Lepus timidus.*

15. *Tetrao lagopus.*

The human implements found in this cavern are of great variety, and of more especial interest than those found in the other caves of the district. They are made of stone, bone, and clay. The most numerous are the cutting flint implements, made solely by hammering; after these in number come the implements which after having been struck off by a blow have had more work bestowed upon them. Some of these may be especially mentioned as having on the sharp edge teeth like a saw. In all Count Zawisza found in this single cavern about two thousand flint implements. In the left side offset or passage was found a single stone celt or axe of serpentine,[1] which was perforated by a circular hole for a handle. It is the only implement of this kind of rock found in any of the caves of the district of Ojcow. Serpentine, as a native rock, does not occur either in the more immediate neighbourhood, or the more distant district around Ojcow. Most likely it came from the neighbourhood of Frankenstein or Jordansmühl in Silesia; this is the more probable as, from numerous discoveries in the last-mentioned place, it is evident that in prehistoric times there was here a manufactory of these objects out of serpentine. The stone celt of diorite, found in the upper cave of Wierszchow, and this serpentine celt are the only two implements of the age of polished stone found in any of the caves of the district of Ojcow.

The implements and ornaments made of bone, horn, and ivory were also plentiful, amongst which more especially may be mentioned borers and smoothing implements; there were also teeth of the cave bear, wolf, fox, and elk, perforated at the root end so as to be worn apparently on a string. The bones of different animals, more particularly of the mammoth, the rhinoceros (*tichorhinus*), the horse and the ox were used for making sharp chisel-shaped tools.

[1] Compare Zawisza, *Caverne de Mammouth*, Plate XIV. Fig. B.

But the most remarkable specimens were those made of ivory; they were of different kinds, and seem to have been rather ornaments than tools. The most curious were some narrow staves or poles, compressed at the sides and sharpened at the end, so that the shape was that of a lancet or a fish. Six or seven of these staves were found. The largest is a foot long and an inch and a half wide in the middle. Some of these staves were dug up in my presence by Count Zawisza, in a bed with charcoal cinders, several feet deep, below the surface of the deposits forming the floor of the cave. Rough flint implements and bones of the reindeer, the wolf, and the polar fox were also found in the same bed. The peculiar structure, viz. the curved lines crossing each other, which characterise ivory, was distinctly recognisable in them. The only question is, whether we may assume that the ivory of these staves came from the tusk of the mammoth (*Elephas primigenius*), or possibly from the tusks of one of the two species of recent elephant. But as numerous remains of the mammoth, more especially the molars, vertebræ, and ribs, were found in the same cave, and as one can hardly imagine a barter trade, by which people of such a low state of civilisation as the makers of these lancet-shaped staves could procure their ivory from Asia or Africa, it seems on the whole probable that these implements were made out of the tusk of the mammoth. Certainly, if we give in to this idea, the further question arises, whether the makers of the staves procured the ivory from the tusks of animals living contemporaneously with them, or whether they had worked up the tusk of some animal which had died before them, the remains of which had been buried in the deposits of the cavern. If we may venture to assume it as proved that, from the results of the cave excavations in France, man and the mammoth lived at the same time, and if we also take into consideration that mammoths' tusks may have been preserved in the ice of Siberia, but could not last so well in damp earth with a changeable temperature, so as to be capable of being worked, it seems as if here also we must conclude that man was contemporaneous with the mammoth. It is not known what was the especial use of these lancet-shaped staves. Possibly they were used as ornaments.

Other specimens made of ivory were no doubt merely ornaments. Amongst this class are small pieces of an oval form, some an inch long, some less, perforated with a round hole at the smaller end; they were probably used as earrings (see Plate IV. Fig. 5). The same thing may be said of a flat-shaped piece, an inch and a half long, perforated with two circular holes, and also ornamented with eight rows of circular hollows (see Plate IV. Fig. 6); also a piece about the length of the finger, perfectly round and sharpened at both ends (see Plate II. Fig. 3). A large rib of the mammoth, forty-six centimetres long, carved at one end so as to form a handle, was probably used as a weapon.

Lastly, amongst the indications of human habitation in this cave there were several fire-places or hearths. They were especially characterised by charcoal ashes and by hard clay, burnt red. Broken bones of animals and flint implements commonly occurred amongst the charcoal. These hearths were found again and again, one over the other, at different levels of the deposit which covers the whole floor of the cave; this deposit is two metres forty-two centimetres thick on the average. In the lowest of the hearths, which was only ten centimetres above the original rock forming the floor of the cave, reindeer antlers, teeth of the cave bear, and mammoth bones were observed amongst the charcoal. In a hearth somewhat higher, probably about the middle of the deposit, were found three molars, and some bones of *Rhinoceros tichorhinus*, and also the mammoth rib before mentioned, one end of which had been worked into a handle. In all the other hearths also, bones and teeth of the mammoth were found, together with reindeer antlers; and Count Zawisza makes the remark that 'the distinction between an older mammoth age and a more recent reindeer period, as made out from the researches in France, will not apply to these Polish caves.' As a general rule, according to the observations of the above-named naturalist, the mammalian and human remains are found exactly the same through the whole thickness of the deposits covering the floor of the cave. The only thing to be remarked is, that in the lowest bed the remains of the cave bear were the most abundant; this animal was almost exclusively the earliest mammalian inhabitant of the cave.

4. THE UPPER CAVE OF WIERSZCHOW.[1]

This cave is about 577 metres from that last described, higher up, in a small valley branching out from the larger one. Count Zawisza has excavated this also, and obtained from it numerous bones of mammalia and human implements. Amongst the animal remains may be especially mentioned the teeth of *Hyæna spelæa*, and the horn core from the horn of a species of antelope, probably that now living in the south of Russia, *Antilope saiga*. Remains were also found of *Ursus spelæus*, *Bos priscus*, *Equus caballus fossilis*, &c.

Implements, and other traces of prehistoric human occupation, were also very numerous. The most interesting specimen is a polished celt of diorite, the only one found in the whole district of Ojcow. Rough flint implements were found in great numbers, as well as pieces of pottery made with the hand alone; the pottery was in general quite rough, while some was ornamented. Bone awls or so-called borers were found here, and ancient fireplaces were also noticed. The floor for about two centimetres thick was made of clay hardened by fire. Close by these hearths were found the rough flint implements.

Two human skulls were found in a narrow hollow at the side of this cave, not far from the entrance, but respecting these Professor Virchow has no remark to make which would indicate either a high antiquity, or in fact any difference from those of the race now inhabiting the district.

[1] In the notices by Count Zawisza it is called simply the cavern of Wierszchow.

5. CAVE ZBÓJECKA (*in German* 'Räuberhöhle').

This cave is situated between Ojcow and the farm of Czajowice, in a woody hollow, which has two precipitous cliffs at the entrance. The footpath between these two places runs through this hollow. The entrance of the cave is on the right side, which is here perpendicular; it is about twenty-five metres above the level of the valley; it opens to the north-west, and is quite low (about forty centimetres only). Immediately within it is wider and develops into a tolerably high arched space, from which a side passage branches both on the left and the right hand. That on the left is short, but that on the right, on the contrary, is 129 metres long, the width being about four metres throughout, but so low as hardly to allow of a man standing upright in it. Thick beds of stalagmite were a hindrance to investigating the deposits covering the floor. Human skulls and bones were particularly abundant in this cave. Sometimes they were found at only a very small depth under the surface, and their state of preservation indicated no high antiquity; others lay deeper in the ground, and some of the bones and skulls were covered with a thick bed of stalagmite, and as they occurred together with ancient bronze implements, a much higher antiquity is to be ascribed to them. The remains of extinct animals in this cave were confined almost entirely to the bones of the cave bear. Lastly, it ought to be mentioned that this cave has only been very partially examined.

6. THE CAVES OF CZAJOWICE.

These caves are in the neighbourhood of the village of Czajowice. The larger of them is only a kilometre and a half distant from the estate of Czajowice, belonging to the Lordship of Ojcow, and is not far from Zbójecka. From the valley in which this cave of Zbójecka is situated, a straight defile leads to the estate of Czajowice. The cave now under consideration is situated in this defile, near where it joins the larger valley. The entrance is to the north, and is about twenty-five metres above the bottom of the gorge. It is two metres high and eighty centimetres wide below. The precipitous slope rises twenty metres above the entrance. A foot-road leading to a lime-kiln runs quite close to it. The floor, immediately on entering the cave, runs steeply downwards, after which the space becomes much larger. On the right side this is continued into a long passage, in which at first a man can stand upright, but when further in becomes so low that one can only creep into it. The whole length of the cave is about 165 metres. More considerable stalagmitic deposits occurred in this cave than in any others which were examined. The roof, the sides, and the floor were covered with it. The front part of the cave, more especially, has the floor covered with a layer of crystalline stalagmite, in some places a foot thick, so that a thorough examination of the cave was rendered more difficult, and the excavations in that part were in consequence somewhat limited. Numerous human remains were found here. In one hearth marked by charcoal, there were found bones of domestic animals, pottery, and implements of iron; a human skeleton was found pressed against the side of the cave at a depth of more than one metre below the surface.

Two other caves in the same hill-slope are of smaller size; one of them lies between that just described, and the Zbójecka cavern; it is about fifteen metres long; the other lies nearer the manor of Czajowice, and can be seen from the road leading to this place. As yet these two caves have only been cursorily examined.

7. THE CAVE OF SADLANA (*in German* '*Schmalzhöhle*').

This cave is in the same valley, and in the same hill-side, as that of Kozarnia, from which it is distant about 400 metres towards the north-east. The chief entrance opens to the east; it is of a triangular form, covered with bushes, and is eighteen metres above the level of the valley. There are also three other openings leading to the inside of the cave; one of them is ten metres above the main entrance, and a winding passage like a fissure connects it with the main cave. Within the chief entrance the floor, which is covered with earth and fragments of rock, runs down very steeply at first, until a space is reached where a man can stand upright. It finishes above in a narrow fissure. Two side passages join this main space. Neither of them, however, have yet been carefully investigated, as the entrances are blocked up by numerous large blocks of stone, which have to be removed before they can be examined. In the larger space, at a depth of three metres, were found numerous bones of recent animals, and also human remains. On the other hand, there were but few bones of extinct animals, the chief of them being those of the cave bear. It ought to be mentioned, however, that this cave has only been very partially excavated, and therefore our ideas about it must be imperfect.

On the same hill-slope, at a distance of three or four hundred metres, there are two other caves, both of which are as it were in fissures. The first is ten metres in length and the other twenty. Neither of them have as yet been excavated.

8. THE CAVES OF BEMBEL ('*Bebel*').

These caves are situated to the north-west of the village of Bembel, on the left slope of the valley, which here is quite flat; further down it becomes deeper, and at last runs into the Bedkowice to the plain of the Rudawa valley. They can be seen from the high road leading from Olkusz to Cracow. The cave of Jerzmanowice lies quite near. A footpath leading from a bridge on the high road to the cave of Jerzmanowice passes quite close to the caves. The first is the larger of the two, and is only half a kilometre from the above-mentioned bridge. The entrance, which is to the north, is in a small rising plain about twelve metres above the bottom of the valley. The cave is small in extent. When the floor was dug up, a fireplace marked by charcoal was found, together with flint flakes, worked flint knives, and numerous pieces of pottery of very rough manufacture. The bones of the cave bear were the only remains of extinct animals found here. But in fact the contents of these caves have not by any means as yet been fully examined.

On the same hill-slope other smaller caves are to be found, similar to those described; but they have not been investigated.

9. The Cave of Górenice.

This cave lies by itself, near the village of Górenice, at some distance westward of those already described. About three kilometres south of this village runs the frontier between Russian Poland and Galicia, and the cave is situated so very near this boundary line, that there may almost be a doubt whether it is situated in Górenice, belonging to the Lordship of Prince Hohenlohe, or to the adjoining Galician monastery of Czerna. The entrances of the cave are to the south, and are situated on the Galician side, at the bottom of a wooded rocky declivity south-east from Górenice, and three kilometres distant from it.

The entrance which was first discovered is 1·40 metre high, and was formerly nearly closed up by great masses of rock lying in front, which have been removed. From this entrance the cave runs for forty metres in a curved form to the second entrance, which like it opens to the south. There are only three places in the cave where one can conveniently stand upright; everywhere else one has to bend or creep. The floor is covered with dark argillaceous earth, and angular pieces of limestone, exactly as in the rest of the caves in the district of Ojcow, and the earth was used for manure in the same way. M. E. Ertel, the inspector of Prince Hohenlohe's estate in Górenice, in the year 1878 sank a pit or shaft in the cave, and obtained from it about 10,000 cwts. of earth; a much larger quantity remains in the cave.

Human remains were very abundant here. Several skulls were found pressed up close to the sides of the cavern. Rough flint implements, and pottery of very coarse manufacture, also occurred, and ancient fireplaces characterised by charcoal were found at various depths from the surface, and in some places were covered with stalagmite. The bones of the cave bear and the molar of a mammoth (*Elephas primigenius*) were the only remains of extinct animals found here; but the skulls and bones of recent animals, more especially the fox and the badger, were very abundant.

LIST OF THE SPECIES OF ANIMALS OF WHICH SKULLS AND BONES HAVE BEEN FOUND IN THE CAVES; AND OF THE HUMAN REMAINS AND IMPLEMENTS.

A. ANIMALS.

1. *Ursus spelæus* (Cave Bear).—Skulls and fragments of skulls, under jaws, teeth, and single bones of many hundred animals.

  a. The greatest skull is 495 millimetres in length and 307 millimetres broad across the zygomatic arch; it belonged to an old animal. (The greatest skull according to Fraas, 'Der Höhlenstein und der Höhlenbär: württemb. nat. Jahresb.' 1862, p. 164, was 496 millimetres long.) Length of the row of molars, about 100 millimetres (according to Fraas, 101 millimetres). The first alveolus is already partly filled up. The last molars, forty-five and forty-six millimetres. Distance from the last molars, measured on the ossa palatina to the lower end, seventy-one millimetres; to the end, sixty-five millimetres. Distance of the two largest cusps of the last molars, 108 millimetres.

  b. Skull of a young animal; the teeth in good preservation, and not worn down; 479 millimetres long and 276 millimetres broad. Length of the row of molars, 103 millimetres. Last molar, fifty-one millimetres. Distance of the two largest cusps of the last molars, 106 millimetres.

  c. The largest molar of the right upper jaw, fifty-six millimetres long (according to Fraas, fifty millimetres), Plate VII. Fig. 2.

  d. The largest canine of the upper jaw, 127 millimetres long. Plate VII. Fig. 1.

  e. The greatest atlas, 242 millimetres wide. Width of the occipital condyle for the epistropheus, ninety-six millimetres (according to Fraas, 242 millimetres, 100 millimetres, ninety-two millimetres).

  f. The greatest humerus, 470 millimetres long (according to Fraas, 460 millimetres).

  g. The greatest femur, 502 millimetres long (according to Fraas, 490 millimetres).

  h. The greatest os penis, 235 millimetres long, Plate VII. Fig. 3 (according to Fraas, 232 millimetres).[1] Plate VII. Fig. 4 gives the drawing of a specimen which had been broken and when healed had been incorrectly joined.

  Localities: Jerzmanowice (very abundant), Kozarnia, Lower Cave of Wierszchow, Zbójecka, Sadlana, Bembel.

---

[1] Professor Owen in his *Anatomy of Vertebrates*, vol. iii. p. 609, says that this bone in '*Ursus arctos* may be six inches in length,' but he adds in a note, 'a fossil specimen of this bone in *Ursus spelæus* measured nine inches,' which agrees with the Polish specimens.—Tr.

2. *Felis spelæa* (Cave Lion).

a. Two imperfect left under jaws, both broken at the alveolus of the canine, and behind the last molars. The specimen drawn (Plate VIII. Fig. 1) has the three molars still perfect, and agrees in size with the under jaw from Bleadon Cavern, drawn by Dawkins and Sanford ('The British Pleistocene Mammalia,' Part I. 1866, Plate I. Fig. 2, Palæontographical Society, vol. xviii.); the length of the row of molars in our specimen is seventy-six millimetres (that drawn by Dawkins and Sanford is seventy-eight millimetres). The distance of the first molar from the alveolar border of the canine in this specimen is somewhat greater than in the English specimen given by Dawkins and Sanford. With respect to the second half under jaw, which apparently belonged to an older animal, the length of the row of molars is seventy-eight millimetres. The first molar has fallen out; the second molar is twenty-eight millimetres long and somewhat worn down. The third tooth is broken away.

b. A left humerus, 363 millimetres long. Burmeister ('Bericht über ein Skelett von Machaerodus,' 1867, p. 16) gives the following measurements of the humerus: *Machærodus*, 380 millimetres; *Felis spelæa*, 380 millimetres; *Felis tigris*, 320 millimetres).

Locality: Jerzmanowice.

c. A very large specimen of the first joint of the third toe of the left fore foot (Plate VIII. Fig. 1, a). The nail sheath is broken off.

Locality: Zbójecka.

d. A perfect first joint of the fourth toe of the right hind foot.

Locality: Zbójecka.

3. *Felis lynx* (the Lynx?) (Plate VIII. Fig. 3).—Left under jaw. The canine and the three molars are in good preservation, the three incisors have fallen out, the *processus coronoideus* is broken off. This specimen agrees well with the fossil under jaw from Issoire (Puy-de-Dôme) drawn by Blainville ('Osteogr.' II. Plate XVI. p. 146), and which he has called *F. issiodorensis*. Length of the row of molars, thirty-seven millimetres. Length of the canine, forty-one millimetres, but measured on the curve of the outside fifty millimetres. The length of the under jaw from the *processus zygomaticus* to the alveolar border of the third incisor is 112 millimetres.

Locality: Sadlana.

4. *Felis catus* (Wild Cat).—Skull in good preservation, but the molars and four incisors are wanting. Length of the skull, 107 millimetres; greatest width of the skull at the temples, forty-nine millimetres.

Locality: Zbójecka.

a. Several specimens of the upper arm bones, which appear too small for *F. lynx*, and which from their appearance belonged to adult animals, ought to be mentioned here. The largest is 128 millimetres long, and the smallest 113 millimetres.

Localities: Górenice, Sadlana.

b. Several fragments of under jaws, some of them nearly perfect. Length of the row of molars, twenty-one to twenty-three millimetres. They 'adhere to the tongue.'

Localities: Kozarnia, Zbójecka, Sadlana, Górenice.

5. *Felis domestica* (Domestic Cat).—Skull the substance of the bone appears very recent, and the skull can hardly be considered actually fossil. This remark will apply to five under jaws, and three specimens of the upper arm bones.

Localities: Jerzmanowice, Sadlana, Zbójecka, Górenice.

6. *Hyæna spelæa* (Cave Hyæna).

a. The halves of two under jaws; a right and a left one from different animals. That drawn (Plate VIII. Fig. 2) is in good preservation, and belonged to a young but fully grown animal. The teeth are not much worn down; the canine was not found in its socket, and yet agrees in size and colour, as well as in the condition of the enamel and mode of wearing, with the specimen now under consideration. Length of the row of molars, ninety-two millimetres. In the other half under jaw only the three molars are preserved; they are stronger than the others which are worn down.

Locality: Jerzmanowice.

b. Two worn-down specimens of the second molar of the right under jaw.

Localities: Jerzmanowice, Kozarnia. According to Count Zawisza, single bones and teeth occur in the Upper Cave of Wierszchow.

7. *Canis lupus* (Wolf).

a. Two left under jaws, in which the incisors, and canines, and the last molar are wanting. In the specimen drawn (Plate IX. Fig. 1) the last molar has fallen out. The distance between the rows of molars from the alveolar border of the last molar to that of the first premolar is 101 millimetres.

Locality: Zbójecka.

The other specimen, which is older, is somewhat smaller; the alveoli of the two last molars are closed up. The distance of the row of molars from the first premolar to the sectorial inclusive, seventy-nine millimetres; in that last described, eighty-four millimetres; in recent specimens, sixty-four millimetres.

Locality: Jerzmanowice.

b. Several imperfect under jaws.

Localities: Jerzmanowice, Zbójecka, Kozarnia, Czajowice.

THE BONE CAVES OF OJCOW.

MEASUREMENTS OF UNDER JAWS IN MILLIMETRES FROM DIFFERENT LOCALITIES.

	Recent	Jerzmanowice	Zbójecka	Czajowice	Kozarnia
Length of the row of molars	80	—	100–101	—	—
Length of the carnassial	24	(1) 29, (2) 31, (3) 30·5 (young)	(1) 30·5, (2) 31, (3) 30·5 (old), (4) 30	31 (very old)	30
Height of the under jaw under the carnassial	32	(1) 32, (2) 32, (3) 30 (young)	(1) 34, (2) 38, (3) 35 (very old), (4) 35	37·5 (very old)	—

c. A fragment of the upper jaw.
Locality : Jerzmanowice.
d. Several portions of the humerus.
Localities : Kozarnia, Zbójecka.

8. *Canis spelæa*.—A species which in the main particulars stands between *Canis lupus* and *Canis vulpes*. The remains before us are from three different caves.

a. On Plate IX. Fig. 2 is a restored drawing of the left under jaw; the incisors and the four first molars are taken from a fragment of the right under jaw, in which only the last molar and the canine are deficient. Length of the jaw, 123 millimetres; that of the row of molars, sixty-six millimetres; the under jaw under the carnassial is twenty-one millimetres in height; length of the carnassial tooth, 21·5 millimetres.
Locality : Kozarnia.

b. Right under jaw. Length of the jaw, 121 millimetres; that of the row of molars, sixty-eight millimetres.
Locality : Jerzmanowice.

c. Right under jaw. The condyles are broken off. Length of the row of molars, sixty-nine millimetres. The last molar has fallen out. Length of the carnassial tooth, twenty-two millimetres. Height of the under jaw below the carnassial, twenty-three millimetres. The second premolar is without cusps, while the third shows one distinctly. In *Canis lupus* there is only one premolar without cusps, but in *Canis vulpes* the three first premolars are without cusps.
Locality : Górenice.

9. *Canis vulpes* (Fox).—Several skulls both perfect and imperfect; numerous under jaws and bones; some of them are decidedly fossil, while others evidently belong to a later period.
Localities : Górenice, Jerzmanowice, Zbójecka, Czajowice, Kozarnia.

10. *Canis lagopus* (Polar Fox).—Five imperfect under jaws. Many more specimens were obtained by Count Zawisza from the cave of Wierszchow.

Localities: Wierszchow, Zbójecka, Kozarnia.

The left under jaw, which is in the best state of preservation, is drawn (Plate IX. Fig. 4), but it wants the incisors, and also the first premolar and the last molar. The measurements do not agree perfectly with those taken from some specimens from Spitzbergen and Greenland; but these latter ones do not agree exactly amongst themselves. A specimen from Spitzbergen is intermediate in the length of the skull between a specimen from Greenland and *Canis vulpes*.

COMPARATIVE MEASUREMENTS OF CANIS VULPES AND CANIS LAGOPUS.

		Length				Height of the under jaw under the carnassial
		Of the skull	Of the under jaws	Of the row of molars	Of the carnassial	
Canis vulpes	Jerzmanowice	142	—	—	—	—
,, ,,	,,	143	—	—	—	—
,, ,,	Silesia ,,	148 (80 mm. broad over the zygomatic arch)	119	60	16	16·5
Canis lagopus	Spitzbergen	121	87	53·5	15	13·5
,, ,,	Greenland	108	82	47	13	12
,, ,,	Zbójecka (specimen drawn)	—	—	52	14	14
,, ,,	Kozarnia	—	—	54·5	14	—
,, ,,	Zbójecka	—	—	—	14·5	14
,, ,,	,,	—	—	—	13·5	14

11. *Meles taxus* (Badger).—Numerous skulls, under jaws, and bones, some of them belonging to a young animal, the teeth being but little worn down. Most of the skulls are decidedly fossil.

Localities: Górenice, Jerzmanowice, Zbójecka, Kozarnia.

12. *Mustela martes* (Marten).

a. Three imperfect skulls, the upper jaws in good preservation. The last premolar has the section crescent-shaped. The carnassial on its outer edge is just as long as the tubercular molar of the upper jaw is broad.

Localities: Jerzmanowice (2), Zbójecka (1).

b. Ten under jaws. The fourth premolar has a second point on the hinder angle of the tooth.

Localities: Zbójecka (3), Kozarnia (4), Sadlana (3).

13. *Fœtorius putorius* (Polecat).—One under jaw, very large.

Locality: Jerzmanowice.

14. *Plecotus auritus* (Long-eared Bat).—Perfect and imperfect skulls, and several under jaws.
Locality: Jerzmanowice.

15. *Vesperugo pipistrellus* (Dwarf Bat).—Numerous bones, imperfect skulls and under jaws.
Locality: Jerzmanowice.

16. *Vesperugo serotinus* (Late-flying Bat).—Two skulls.
Locality: Jerzmanowice.

17. *Vespertilio murinus* (Common Bat).—Numerous skulls and bones.
Locality: Jerzmanowice.

18. *Talpa europæa* (Mole).—Three under jaws, two humerus, one femur, four pelvis, one cuboideum, one tibia.
Locality: Jerzmanowice.

19. *Erinaceus europæus* (Hedgehog).—Eighteen under jaws, several imperfect skulls and bones.
Locality: Zbójecka.

20. *Sorex vulgaris* (Shrew).—Perfect and imperfect skulls.
Locality: Zbójecka.

21. *Cervus tarandus* (Reindeer).—Portions of the antlers, and imperfect under jaws and bones, are now before us. The antlers belonged to animals of very different ages. The largest fragment is 0·64 millimetre long, and it measures 0·06 millimetre in diameter at the bottom. It was found at Kozarnia. The distance of the 'brow antler' from the second tyne is 0·67 millimetre, and the distance from this to the third, which runs backwards, is 0·31. The horn of a much younger animal is drawn in Plate XI. Fig. 2, while that drawn in Plate XII. Fig. 2 belonged to an animal still younger. In both these cases the lower end is perfectly flat and even, and several other specimens are in the same condition, so that all these have been naturally shed by the animals. In some instances the lower end of the horn is still connected with a piece of the skull, which shows that the animal died a violent death.
Localities: Kozarnia, Jerzmanowice, Zbójecka, Górenice, Bembel.

22. *Cervus alces* (Elk).
a. Imperfect under jaw.
Locality: Sadlana.

b. A molar tooth.
Locality: Kozarnia.
c. Numerous bones and pieces of antlers.
Localities: Lower Cave of Wierszchow; 'Mammoth Cave,' according to Count Zawisza.

23. *Cervus elaphus* (Red Stag).—Several fragments of antlers, under jaw, also worked pieces of antlers.
Localities: Jerzmanowice, Kozarnia, Górenice, Wierszchow, Saspow.

24. *Cervus capreolus* (Roebuck).—An imperfect skull with the bases of the antlers.
Localities: Górenice, Zbójecka. Count Zawisza has also found it at Wierszchow, but rarely.

25. *Ovis sp.* (Sheep).—Numerous under jaws and single teeth; the state of preservation, however, does not indicate any high antiquity.
Localities: Zbójecka, Sadlana, Jerzmanowice.

26. *Capra sp.* (Goat).—Apparently not quite fossil.
Locality: Górenice.

27. *Antilope saiga?*—A single horn-core was found by Count Zawisza, probably of the species which is now living wild in the south of Russia.
Locality: Upper cave of Wierszchow.

28. *Bos primigenius.*—The half of a right under jaw, broken off behind. The premolars are perfect, and in good preservation. The last molar (Plate X. Fig. 1) agrees in size and form with the specimens drawn by Rütimeyer ('Versuch einer natürlichen Geschichte des Rindes,' Taf. II. Fig. 2).
Locality: Kozarnia.

29. *Bos taurus* (Domestic Ox).—Numerous imperfect skulls and under jaws, single teeth and bones. Most of them apparently only partially fossil.

30. *Bos priscus.*
a. A left metacarpus from the cave of Jerzmanowice (Plate XI. Fig. 1) agrees with that drawn by Nordmann (l.c. Taf. XVI. Fig. 2), and referred to by him as *Bos priscus*. The bone under consideration is 232 millimetres long (231 Nordmann); it measures in breadth 94 millimetres at the upper end (86 Nordmann), in the middle 61 millimetres (59 Nordmann), and at the lower end 97 millimetres (92 Nordmann).
b. A second metacarpus from Kozarnia is more slender in form. It is 244 millimetres

long, 85 millimetres broad at the upper end, and 49 millimetres in the middle; a piece has been broken off the lower end, so that the breadth there can only be estimated at 70 to 80 millimetres.

c. Count Zawisza says that bones of this animal have been found in the cave of Wierszchow

31. *Equus fossilis.*

a. An imperfect left under jaw; the last and third molars are in place, also several loose teeth.

Locality: Sadlana.

b. Three terminal phalanges. That drawn (Plate X. Fig. 4 and 4a) from the cave of Jerzmanowice is of considerable size, 100 millimetres broad. Two others from Jerzmanowice and Kozarnia are only 76 millimetres broad.

c. A middle phalanx bone from the cave of Jerzmanowice, 95 millimetres in length.

32. *Elephas primigenius* (Mammoth).

a. Four molars.

Localities; Kozarnia (2), Wierszchow (1), Jerzmanowice (1).

b. The point of the tusk of a young animal (Plate X. Fig. 3).

Locality: Zbójecka.

c. Weathered pieces of ivory.

Locality: Kozarnia.

d. A scapula, and some other pieces of bone.

Locality: Jerzmanowice.

33. *Rhinoceros tichorhinus s. antiquitatis.*—A piece of the left upper jaw with the two last molars in good preservation; fragment of the fifth molar of the left under jaw; the left milk tooth, and an imperfect molar of the upper jaw (Plate X. Fig. 2).

Locality: Kozarnia.

34. *Sus scrofa* (Wild Boar).

Numerous imperfect under jaws, chiefly of young boars, and also some of very old animals, with the crowns of the teeth almost entirely worn down, also bones and single teeth.

Localities: Wierszchow, Jerzmanowice, Kozarnia, Zbójecka, Sadlana, Bembel, Górenice.

35. *Sus sp.*—Several skulls, as determined by Rutimeyer, belong to the woolly-haired East 'European Asiatic' race (Domestic breed). Only half-fossil.

Locality: Górenice.

36. *Lepus vulgaris* (Hare).—Imperfect skulls, and numerous bones of the extremities.
Localities: Jerzmanowice, Zbójecka, Górenice.

37. *Lepus variabilis*, as determined by Professor Liebe of Gera.—Bones of the extremities.
Localities: Zbójecka, Górenice.

38. *Myodes torquatus* (Collared Lemming), as determined by Professor Dr. Nehring.—Two under jaws.
Locality: Jerzmanowice.

39. *Myodes lemmus, var. Obensis*, as determined by Professor Dr. Nehring.—An imperfect skull, and a right under jaw.
Locality: Jerzmanowice.

40. *Sciurus vulgaris* (common Squirrel).—An under jaw.
Locality: Jerzmanowice.

41. *Myoxus glis* (Dormouse).—An imperfect skull, two under jaws, and a humerus.
Locality: Jerzmanowice.

42. *Cricetus frumentarius* (Hamster).—An imperfect skull, with all the teeth preserved, a genuine fossil under jaw.
Locality: Jerzmanowice.

43. *Mus sylvaticus* (Wood-mouse), as determined by Professor Dr. Nehring.—Some imperfect skulls, numerous under jaws, and two tibiæ.
Locality: Jerzmanowice.

44. *Arvicola (Hypudæus) glareolus* (Great-headed Field-mouse), as determined by Professor Dr. Nehring.—Two imperfect skulls, and numerous under jaws.
Locality: Jerzmanowice.

45. *Arvicola (Hypudæus) amphibia* (Water-rat).—Hundreds of imperfect skulls, under jaws and bones, some of them actually fossil, others with the substance of the bone but little changed.
Localities: Jerzmanowice, Kozarnia, Sadlana.

46. *Arvicola ratticeps* (Rat), as determined by Professor Dr. Nehring.—One imperfect skull, with under jaws in good condition.
Locality: Jerzmanowice.

47. *Arvicola arvalis* (Field-mouse), as determined by Professor Dr. Nehring.—Imperfect skulls and under jaws.
Locality: Jerzmanowice.

48. *Arvicola agrestis* (Short-tailed mouse).—Four imperfect skulls.

49. *Syrnium aluco* (the little Owl).—A metatarsus. This has been determined by Professor Liebe, and also the following species of birds.
Locality: Kozarnia.

50. *Merula torquata* (a Femur).
Locality: Kozarnia.

51. *Fringilla linota.*—Imperfect skull.
Locality: Jerzmanowice.

52. *Fringilla conf. carduelis.*—Imperfect skull.
Locality: Jerzmanowice.

53. *Emberiza sp.*—Imperfect skull.
Locality: Jerzmanowice.

54. *Corvus cornix.*—One humerus, a very large specimen, approaching *C. segetum*.
Locality: Jerzmanowice.

55. *Garrulus glandarius.*—The under and upper jaw of one bird.
Locality: Jerzmanowice.

56. *Hirundo sp.*—One humerus.
Locality: Jerzmanowice.

57. *Tetrao urogallus* (Capercailzie).
a. An under jaw, an imperfect skull, a humerus, breastbone, and vertebræ.
Locality: Zbójecka.
b. An upper jaw.
Locality: Jerzmanowice.
c. A metatarsus.
Locality: Czajowice.
d. A cubitus.
Locality: Sadlana.

58. *Perdix cinerea* (Partridge).—A humerus.
Locality: Sadlana.
Four metatarsals of a very small race.
Locality: Jerzmanowice.

59. *Gallus domesticus* (Domestic Fowl).—Numerous bones of the extremities of at least three races.
Localities: Zbójecka, Górenice, Sadlana, Kozarnia.

60. *Anser* (Goose).—Cervical vertebra.
Locality: Sadlana.

61. *Bufo sp.*—Numerous remains.
Locality: Jerzmanowice.

62. *Rana temporaria.*—One humerus.
Locality: Jerzmanowice.

B. HUMAN REMAINS AND IMPLEMENTS.

I. SKULLS AND BONES.

A number of skulls and bones were found in the different caves. It is evident, however, that these human remains belong to very different ages. Unfortunately, when they were found, the different animal remains occurring with them were not in every case accurately noted. But that man, at any rate for a time, was contemporaneous with animals now extinct, more especially with the cave bear, may be considered as certain. Attention is particularly called to the fact already mentioned on p. 9, that on the lower surface of a great piece of stalagmite was fixed a vertebra of the cave bear and also a flint implement evidently made by human hands. The human skulls found in the caves have been examined by Geh. Rath Professor Dr. Virchow.[1]

Some time since he examined certain skulls sent to him by Count Zawisza from the cave of Wierszchow, 'Mammoth cave.' (See Verh. der 'Zeitschrift für Ethnologie,' Bd. V. S. 192.) With respect to two of them, he remarked, that although Count Zawisza is inclined to date them back to the age of polished stone (neolithic), yet it seemed to him probable that they were comparatively more recent, and possibly might be ' of Sclavonic origin.'

---

[1] Although in my younger days I paid some attention to comparative anatomy, yet several of the terms used by Professor Virchow in these papers are new to me. Consequently, to prevent any mistake, I ventured to ask my friend, Professor W. Boyd Dawkins, to revise the nomenclature of my translation of Professor Virchow's papers; this he has kindly consented to do, so that I send the MS. to the printers with confidence.—TR

Subsequently, Professor Virchow wrote as follows respecting a skull sent to him by me from the cave of Górenice ('Verhandl. der Berlin. Gesellsch. für Anthropologie, Ethnologie und Urgeschichte,' Jahrg. 1879, S. 12 g. Mit Taf. IV.).

At the meeting on December 6, 1873 (Verh. S. 192, 'Zeitschr. für Ethnol.' Bd. V.) I exhibited human remains from the bone caves of Cracow sent to me by Count Zawisza.

It seems doubtful whether one of the caves examined by Dr. Roemer is identical with the above or not. In a paper given April 24, 1878, to the Silesian Association for the advancement of the country's science, he mentions the cave as that of Wierzbanowice, south of Olkusz in Poland. And he adds that it is situated between Olkusz and Ojcow. On the skull sent to me there is a label Górenice, so that one may probably conclude that it refers to another cave in the same neighbourhood.

As appears from Professor Roemer's letter even the exact locality in the cave is not quite certain; the depth at which it was found is in itself not decisive, as we cannot get rid of the possibility that after the older beds were deposited, human bodies may have been brought and interred there. On this point I do not forget my own communications on Riunekaln in Livland (Sitzung vom 20. October 1877, S. 407, 'Zeitschr. für Ethnol.' Bd. IX. S. 407); nor my paper on the skeleton found in the bears' cave of Aggtelek in Upper Hungary (Sitzung vom 21. Juli 1877, S. 316). Most certainly it requires very careful examination not only of the deposit in which a skeleton is found, but also of the particular condition of the beds covering it, to enable us to decide whether it is younger or older.

Everything about the skull sent to me appears to go against its high antiquity. It has, strictly speaking, nothing fossil about it. It is not only on the whole in good preservation, but in some few places it appears quite recent. The surface is very smooth and close or solid, the beds or layers of bone adhere well together, there is the want of 'adherence to the tongue,' and the condition of the bone is firm but not heavy; all these facts indicate an interment of a more recent age. Some dendritical markings on the left side do not at all invalidate such a theory. On the right side the colour is more brown.

Although unfortunately I had no drawing taken of the skull previously examined, and though I can only compare the two from the description then given by me, yet I think I am correct in saying that the skull now before us stands both ethnologically and chronologically near the two which were previously examined. The measurements taken are complete enough to guarantee a correct decision. In order, however, to obtain a more secure foothold for the future, I give on Plate IV. the geometrical drawings of the skull of Górenice reduced to one-third of the natural size.

The skull belonged to a woman in middle life; the well-worn teeth, and the great number of synostoses, are in favour of this conclusion. On both sides there is a synostosis of the spheno-frontal and the lower part of the coronal sutures. The spheno-parietal suture (in its front portion) is also in part completely obliterated on each side of the masto-occipital suture, but on the left side a trace appears of the transverse occipital suture.

The skull is long and low, with a flat occiput, but behind the coronal suture the curve of the crown is somewhat more decided and the occiput more projecting; the forehead is upright but low, the tubera strongly developed. The appearance of the face is, moreover, very striking. On the whole it is low, the orbits are very characteristic, being broad and low, though at the same time they are deep. The nose also is short and broad with a deeply sunk ridge. The alveolar apophysis of the upper jaw is also low but slightly prognathous. The under jaw is wanting.

The following are the chief measurements:

	Millimetres
Greatest length	187
Greatest breadth	132
Perpendicular height	126
Auricular height	108
Lower frontal width (*Untere Stirnbreite*)	96
Temporal diameter (*Temporaldurchmesser*)	116
Parietal diameter (*Parietaldurchmesser*)	120
Occipital diameter (*Occipitaldurchmesser*)	105
Mastoideal diameter, at base (*Mastoidealdurchmesser, Basis*)	114
Auricular diameter (*Auriculardurchmesser*)	104
Height of the upper face (from the root of the nose to the alveolar border)	57
Breadth of the face (*Sut. Zygom. maxill.*)	93
Height of the nose	43
Breadth of the nasal aperture	24
Height of the orbits	29
Breadth of the orbits	41

To the index numbers taken from the above measurements I append, for the sake of comparison, those of the two skulls from Wierszchow previously exhibited by me. The result shows decided similarity (on the whole) and but slight differences.

	Górcalce	Wierszchow	
		I.	II.
	♀	♂	♂
Index of length and breadth or cephalic index (*Längenbreiten-Index*)	70·5	73·5	75·4
Index of length and height (*Längenhöhen-Index*)	67·3	80·4	—
Index of breadth and height (*Breitenhöhen-Index*)	95·4	102·3	—
Auricular height Index (*Ohrhöhen-Index*)	57·7	—	—
Nasal Index (*Nasen-Index*)	55·8	46	47
Orbital Index (*Orbital-Index*)	70·7	75	79·5
Upper face Index (*Obergesichts-Index*)	61·2	—	—

Unfortunately, in the year 1873, I did not take the auricular height (*Ohrhöhe*) nor the breadth of the face (*Gesichtsbreite*) (the distance between the two zygomatic maxillary sutures), so that these measurements cannot be obtained. However, as I then made out the form of the face in both the skulls from Wierszchow showed greater similarity than the above measurements, notwithstanding both of them were dolichocephalic.

We now see that the female skull of Górenice is still more dolichocephalic than the male skull of Wierszchow No. I.; although, unlike it, it is low. The complete dolichocephalic character is, in my opinion, no objection to its Sclavonic origin, as I have frequently and repeatedly made the distinction. With respect to the face not only is the small height remarkable in all three cases, but the low numbers of the orbital index are very striking. Even the Wierszchow skull No. II., although it has the highest measurement, is yet far below the average of most European skulls. In both the Wierszchow skulls the nose is leptorrhine, while in the Górenice skull it is platyrrhine. But a difference like this is often found between the sexes, and is seen here in the extreme lowness of the female nose, while the breadth of the nasal aperture is similar in all the three skulls.

It is interesting to compare them with the skulls from Aggtelek, a cave on the southern side of the mountain range of Galician Hungary, as even here there was a mixture of both brachy- and meso-cephalic forms, and there were also decided dolichocephalic ones, some of which were leptorrhine and mesorrhine.

Although we can by no means consider it probable that any one of the skulls from the caves of the Ojcow valley belongs to the age of the mammoth, yet this does not affect the question of the co-existence of man with the mammoth in this district. Professor Roemer, at the meeting of the Silesian Institute on November 20, 1878, said that Count Zawisza had excavated in his presence from a bed with charcoal in the mammoth cave of Wierszchow 'several thin rods pressed together at the sides and sharpened at the ends, lancet-shaped and fish-like in form, the largest of which was one foot long and one and one-eighth inch broad.' They were made of ivory, and in fact, as Professor Roemer states, of mammoth ivory. In the same bed were found worked palæozoic flints, and bones of the reindeer, polar fox, mammoth, &c.

Professor Virchow evidently does not consider this skull as very old, and from his remarks there is nothing striking about it. He subsequently communicated the following observations on five other skulls found in different caves near Ojcow, which had been sent to him for examination.[1]

On Cave Skulls from the District of the Upper Vistula.

In continuation of my previous communications (Sitzung vom 6. December, 1878, Verhandl. S. 192, 'Zeitschr. für Ethnol.' Bd. V. und Sitzung vom 11. Januar, 1879, Verhandl. S. 9, 'Zeitschr.' Bd. XL), I now exhibit again a series of human skulls from the prehistoric caves of the district of the Upper Vistula. They form a part of the result of the excavations under the superintendence of Professor Roemer, of Breslau. One of them, 'Górenice No. I.,' has been

---

[1] Verhandl. der Berl. Gesellsch. für Anthropologie, Ethnologie und Urgeschichte, Jahrg. 1880, S. 52-55.

already described by me, last year; the other five are new to us. Of these, two came also from the cave of Górenice, near Ojcow: one has the label Czajowice (2), and two others are marked Zbójecka, Nos. 1 and 2. Nothing definite is known to me as to the situation of these different localities one to another. However, the skulls themselves seem to differ extremely; while that from Górenice is covered in parts with uncommonly thick black dendritic markings, not a trace of anything of the kind is to be seen on the skulls from Czajowice and Zbójecka. Again, the bones from the last two places are light and fragile and of a clear yellowish colour, while those from the first appear heavier, more solid, and more grey, and consequently have the appearance of being older.

There is a little difficulty in comparing the skulls one with another, as three of them belonged to young persons, viz. that from Górenice No. 2, that from Czajowice, and that from Zbójecka No. 2, and also because the difference of sex must be taken into consideration. With respect to the Górenice skull No. 3, and that from Czajowice, it is doubtful to which sex they are to be attributed. The two other skulls from Górenice, according to all appearance, are female, while that from Zbójecka is that of a male.

Then, again, there are numerous parts damaged and wanting. The Górenice skull No. 3 is the worst in this respect; for in this only the crown of the skull has been preserved. The list of measurements will show where the other skulls are defective. In that from Czajowice the face has been partly restored; but still not so completely as to prevent the measurements for the nose orbits and palates from being relied on with certainty. The skull from Czajowice was the only one found which had the under jaw perfect.

It appears, therefore, to me that in explaining this 'find,' I ought to be very careful, and I shall restrict myself entirely to the average measurements.

The individual peculiarities of the skulls may be taken as follows:

1. This skull has already been described; I have only to add that the hinder part of the circumference of the for. magn. occip. is much injured, that the supra-occipital bone projects very far back, and the protub. occip., which is very faint, is situated far forward and low down; that, further, there is some stenokrotaphy, the frontal margins are very smooth, the nasal ridge alone is rather more arched, and lastly, that the fossæ caninæ are very deeply hollowed out (*ausgebuchtet*).

The skull No. 2 from Górenice is that of a young woman. The synchondr. spheno-occip. are not yet closed; the wisdom teeth have not yet come up, and the crowns of the other teeth retain their sharp points. Moreover, it is very like the skull No. 1, as the indices will show. This decidedly dolichocephalic and low skull, in which the sutures are all open and moderately dentated, has an upright low forehead, a long and flat crown of the head, and the occiput widely spread, only the tubera are more strongly developed. The face is low; the nose is short, the ridges of which are somewhat broad, and very much curved inwards; the alveolar process of the upper jaw is very low, and yet somewhat prognathous; the orbits are low with the upper borders almost straight; the palate, short and broad, almost the shape of a horseshoe.

3. The crown of the skull, which is all that remains of No. 3 from Góreniec. Although the bone is thick, and evidently belonged to an older individual, it is yet comparatively light and uncertain as to sex. The forehead is tolerably upright, low, and with small supra-orbital ridges; the tubera are well developed; the sutures strongly dentated. At the top of the lambdoid suture, and at the back part of the sagittalis, and also at the back part of the spheno-temporal suture, there are intercalated bones. The alæ large; the upper squamous bone is bent out considerably; the crown broadly and considerably arched; the mastoid processes but weakly developed; the flat part of the occipital foramen raised up obliquely behind; the index is mesocephalic, on account of its considerable height.

The skull from Czajowice is quite that of a young person. The spheno-occipital suture is open; the bone is thin; the teeth are changing, and the dog tooth has not yet come through. There is in consequence great irregularity near the lambdoid suture; there is a great 'os apicis,' nearly of a quadratic form, twenty-five millimetres high and thirty millimetres broad, somewhat diagonal, intercalated far into the sagittal suture, which makes a great bend towards the right emissarium, and here is quite simple, while the left emissarium is of very small size. The effect of this is seen in the measurements of the sagittal curve. The skull is proportionably high and decidedly mesocephalic; the highest part being in the region of the fontanelle. The forehead is low but full; the upper squamous scale is strongly bent outwards. The palate is short, moderately broad and deep. The under jaw with low projections; the side pieces are somewhat thick; the chin projects; the teeth are somewhat awry.

5. The skull from Zbójecka No. 1 is that of a male, hypsidolicho-cephalic, yet approaches nearly to meso-cephalic. The bone is thick but light, and it is in good preservation, excepting near the left os petrosum (*Felsenbein*); there is also a small artificial deficiency at the hinder edge of the occipital foramen. The ridge of the nose is strong—there are the remains of a sut. frontalis very much dentated, and also a slight indication of a crista frontalis; consequently it projects somewhat in the middle, and is very much arched towards the nose. Moreover, it is long, and bent a trifle backwards. On the right it rises from the for. supra-orbitale from a deep furrow. The tubera are low. The middle of the skull is high and broad. The upper squamous bone of the occiput projects strongly, the protuberance lies far in front. On the right there is a trace of the sut. transversa occipitis. The cerebellar pits are strongly arched outside. The proc. condyloides are very large, with a decided curve of the articular facets. The plane of the occipital foramen produced behind; the mastoid processes are small. The cheek-bones strongly marked. The face is longer than in the skulls before described, but yet with broad cheek-bones, consequently giving a more moderate index of the

F

face. Orbits rather quadranglar and yet low. Nose narrow, with a narrow prominent ridge, and in consequence decidedly leptorrhine. The alveolar process higher. The alveoli of the missing incisors large. The remaining teeth large and but little worn down. Palate large and wide.

6. The skull from Zbójecka No. 2, though belonging to a young person, is probably that of a male. The spheno-occipital suture is open, the wisdom teeth have not come through, the crowns of the teeth are not worn, the bone is thin; unfortunately it is much damaged, but it is a great broad skull of meso-cephalic form (Index 78. 1). The forehead is very flat and full, with traces of a crista front., and distinct tubera. A large and long curve of the crown. On the right side there is inserted a 'Wormian' bone in the upper part of the lambdoid suture, which here bends considerably; it consists of four adjoining parts, the uppermost being thirty-three millimetres long and twenty millimetres broad; the second three millimetres long and twenty-two millimetres broad; the third eight millimetres long and twenty-eight millimetres broad; the fourth eight millimetres long and twenty-six millimetres broad. The line of division between these bones is quite straight. On the left the beginning of the sut. transv. occip. is preserved. The cerebellar arches are large. The mastoid processes are small. The face differs considerably. The orbits are high (Index 89. 4), the nose long, narrow, with very projecting roots and prominent ridges, consequently leptorrhine (Index 44). Narrow cheek-bones, consequently a greater index of the face (74.4 millimetres). Alveolar process shorter and, on account of the size of the alveoli of the incisors, slightly prognathous. Very large horseshoe-shaped palate, with an index of 88.3.

The following tables give the exact measurements:

I. ACTUAL MEASUREMENTS.

	Górenice			Cmajowice (?)	Zbójecka	
	1 ♀	2 ♀	3 ♂	4 ♂	5 ♂	6 ♂
Greatest length	187	184·5	178·2	176	184	183
Greatest breadth	132	132	140	139	139	143
Greatest height	126	119	135	132	142	137
Height of ear	108	103	112	117	116	115
Horizontal circumference	505	—	504	489	501	514
Vertical oblique circumference	295	—	298	305	302	—
Sagittal circumference						
Forehead	120	117	118	126	122	131
Sagittal suture	128	120	125	105[1]	135	123
Occiput	—	119	112	142[1]	—	109
Entire arch (see three last measurements) (*Gesammtbogen*)	—	356	355	373	—	363
Breadth of the lower forehead	96	—	95·5	89	96	96·5
Breadth of the temple (*Schläfenbreite*)	116	—	116	105	114	—
Parietal breadth	120	125	131	134	130	136
Occipital breadth	105	100	103·5	102	107	—
Auricular breadth	104	—	113	96	115	—

[1] Intercalated bones.

I. ACTUAL MEASUREMENTS—continued.

	Górenice			Czajowice (2)	Zbójecka	
	1 ♀	2 ♀	3 ♂	4 ♂	5 ♂	6 ♂
Mastoideal breadth (base)	114	—	121	108	123	—
Mastoideal breadth (point)	—	—	—	90·5	103	—
Jugal (*Jugalbreite*)	—	—	—	—	136	122
Breadth at the angle of the lower jaw (*Unterkieferwinkelbreite*)	—	—	—	85	—	—
Breadth of the malar (*bizygom.*)	93	—	—	—	94	88
Base root of nose:						
(*a*) Ear aperture	103	94	100	90·5	102	98·5
(*b*) Occipital foramen	98	93	99	85·5	102·5	98
Nasal spine:						
(*a*) Ear aperture	104	96	—	—	108	98·5
(*b*) Occipital foramen	90·5	98	—	—	94	89·5
Alveolar border:						
(*a*) Ear aperture	107·5	102	—	—	112	104
(*b*) Occipital foramen	94	92	—	—	95·5	93
Chin:						
(*a*) Ear aperture	—	—	—	—	—	—
(*b*) Occipital foramen	—	—	—	—	—	—
Height of face:						
(*a*) Chin	—	—	—	100	—	—
(*b*) Alveolar border	57	55	—	56	63	65·5
Orbits:						
Height	29	28·5	—	—	33	34
Breadth	41	37	—	—	43	38
Nose:						
Height	43	45	—	—	50	50
Breadth	24	24	—	—	22	22
Alveolar border	10	10	—	11	13	11
Palate:						
Length	—	43	—	—	47	43
Breadth	—	33	—	—	37	—

II. INDICES.[1]

	Górenice			Czajowice (2)	Zbójecka	
	1 ♀	2 ♀	3 ♂	4 ♂	5 ♂	6 ♂
Cephalic Index (*Längenbreiten-Index*)	70·5	71·7	78·7	79	75·5	78·1
Index of height (*Längenhöhen-Index*)	67·3	64·7	75·8	75	77·2	74·9
Index of breadth and height (*Breitenhöhen-Index*)	95·4	90·1	96·4	94·9	102·1	95·8
Auricular Index (*Ohrhöhen-Index*)	57·7	55·8	62·8	66·4	63·0	62·8
Nasal Index (*Nasen-Index*)	55·8	51·0	—	—	44·0	44·0
Orbital Index (*Orbital-Index*)	70·7	77·0	—	—	76·7	89·4
Facial Index (*Gesichts-Index*)	61·2	—	—	—	67	74·4
Palatal Index (*Gaumen-Index*)	—	76·7	—	—	78·7	88·3

[1] Some of these indices, according to my calculation, differ very slightly from those of Professor Virchow: the figures, however, are copied *exactly* from those in Professor Roemer's book. Anyone who wishes to study the matter more accurately can easily refer to the papers of Professor Virchow. As his terms in some cases appear to differ from those of English anthropologists, it has been thought desirable to add the original German words in italics.—Tr.

II. Implements.

a. MADE FROM STONE AND GLASS.

1. Flint implements for cutting purposes, made solely by being struck or forced off from a larger core, and very slightly if at all worked up afterwards. They are generally about the length of a finger, and an inch in width, and are in shape like a flake or chip with a sub-parallel cutting edge. They are found of various sizes, both small and large, and some of them are very irregular in shape (see Plate I. Figs. 3, 4, 5, and 8). The nuclei or cores, as they call the larger pieces of flint from which the flakes are struck off by skilful strokes, are also found in considerable abundance.

Localities: Jerzmanowice (very plentiful), Kozarnia, Bembel, Sadlana, Zbójecka, Czajowice, Wierszchow.

Count Zawisza has published numerous drawings of these flint implements found in the two caves of Wierszchow ('Rech. Archéol. en Pologne,' Taf. iii. iv. v. vi. vii. viii. ix. x. xv. xvi. xvii. xviii. and xix.).

2. Cutting flint implements, also made by being struck off from a larger mass of flint, but afterwards worked into a regular form (not ground down or polished). In general they are pieces of a lengthened elliptic or lancet-shaped form, one side of which is flat and the other convex. The convex side is formed by two planes meeting in a ridge in the middle (arrow-heads, lance-heads) (see Plate I. Figs. 6, 7, and 9). One specimen, with a notched and dentated edge, has apparently been used as a saw (see Plate I. Fig. 2).

3. Stone axes or celts. Only two of these were found in the whole of the caves of the district of Ojcow; in fact they were discovered by Count Zawisza in the caves of Wierszchow. One is a stone axe of serpentine perforated with a circular hole to receive a handle; it was found in the lower cave of Wierszchow (the so-called 'Mammoth cave'): the other, which was of diorite, was found in the upper cave of Wierszchow. Both have been rubbed down smooth. They are the only 'polished' stone implements which have ever been noticed in any of the caves near Ojcow.

4. Corn crushers, that is, roundish, cuboidal stones, the size of a man's fist, which have generally been thought to have been used for crushing corn. Several of them are now before us, from the cave of Jerzmanowice. We may especially refer to one of diorite; two of the surfaces are considerably worn down (see Plate V. Fig. 11).

5. Polishers, or rubbers of various kinds of stone, apparently for making the bone implements. We have several now before us from the caves of Kozarnia and Zbójecka. Some

are of fine grained sandstone, and others of black clay slate (see Plate V. Figs. 8, 9, 10*a*, and 10*b*).

6. Amber beads, rather flat, and not perfectly round, but smoothed. Three specimens were found in the cave of Zbójecka (see Plate V. Figs. 3 and 4).

7. Glass beads with inlaid threads of clear-coloured glass, similar to those now made at Venice (see Plate V. Figs. 1 and 2). The occurrence of these beads in the deeper beds of the floor of the caves, as well as the decided 'weathering' of the surface, induce us to attribute to them a great antiquity. The art required to make these beads excludes the possibility of their having been made by the ancient inhabitants of the cave, and thus indicates most decidedly that they are of foreign origin.

Locality: two specimens, both from the cave of Kozarnia.

b. SPECIMENS MADE FROM BONE.

1. *Tools.*

1. Rods or staves artificially sharpened at one end, which apparently have been used as borers or awls (Plate II. Figs. 4, 8, 9, 10, 12; Plate III. Figs. 2, 3, 4, 6). Some of them are perforated at the broader end (Plate II. Fig. 13, Plate III. Fig. 5).

2. A knife made of the lower tusk of a wild boar; half of it has been so ground down that the enamel of the tooth forms the cutting edge of the knife (see Plate IV. Fig. 8). Only one single specimen is before us; it was found in the cave of Jerzmanowice.

3. A flat-shaped piece of bone, a foot long, gradually sharpened at the point; its use is unknown (Plate II. Fig. 1). Only one specimen was found; it came from the cave of Jerzmanowice.

4. A barbed arrow head (Plate IV. Fig. 11). Only one single specimen was found, and it came from the cave of Jerzmanowice.

5. A sewing needle with an eye at the top. We have only obtained one specimen, and this is broken (Plate IV. Fig. 10). It was found in the cave of Kozarnia.

6. A canine tooth of the cave bear, perforated with a round hole at the lower end. Its use is unknown, but it probably was worn on a string (Plate IV. Fig. 7). It was found in the cave of Zbójecka.

7. Straight hollow birds' bones, cut off transversely at one end, and broken off at the other. The use is unknown (see Plate IV. Fig. 13). From the cave of Zbójecka.

Count Zawisza has drawn a somewhat similar specimen from the cave of Wierszchow ('Mammoth cave'); it is ornamented with neat transverse lines (see 'Rech. Archéol. en Pologne,' Warszawa 1874, Taf. XI. Fig. 2).

2. *Objects for Ornament, Amulets, or Games.*

1. An ivory rod sharpened at both ends, as regularly round as if turned in a lathe, and with a hollow furrow round the middle of it; it is straight and prettily ornamented (see Plate II. Fig. 2, copied from Count Zawisza's figure, Plate XI. Fig. 1).

2. Ivory rods, compressed, lancet-shaped, or of the form of a fish (see Plate II. Fig. 2, copied from Count Zawisza). The largest of them is one foot long, and in the middle it is an inch and a half broad. Seven of these rods were discovered by Count Zawisza in the lower cave of Wierszchow ('Mammoth cave'). They were found together in a bed with charcoal and rough flint implements, and bones of the wolf, the reindeer, and the polar fox.

3. Oval pieces of ivory an inch long, or less, narrower at one end and there perforated; they probably may have been ear pendants (Plate IV. Fig. 5). Several specimens were found with this one just described, and in the same cave.

4. A flat piece an inch and a half long, perforated with two circular holes (Plate IV. Fig. 6), and also ornamented with seven rows of circular depressions. This was found by Count Zawisza in the same place, and has been drawn by him.

5. A rectangular flat plate of bone, an inch in length, perforated with six circular holes (Plate IV. Fig. 1). From the cave of Sadlana.

6. Small rhomboidal plate of bone, perforated in the middle, the surface is ornamented (?) with scratches of uncertain character (see Plate IV. Fig. 4).

7. Small triangular plate of bone, made out of the os hyoides of a large ruminant (see Plate IV. Fig. 3).

8. Tusk of a wild boar ground down flat on one side, and perforated at each end with a round hole (Plate IV. Fig. 2). It probably was worn on a string as a neck ornament. This unique specimen was from the cave of Czajowice.

9. Canine teeth of the wolf and fox perforated at the end (Count Zawisza, l.c. Taf. XI. Figs. 8 and 9). Several specimens were found in the cave of Wierszchow.

10. Incisor of elk, also perforated at the root end (Count Zawisza, l.c. Taf. XI. Fig. 5). From the same cave.

11. Bone beads, but imperfectly rounded and smoothed (Plate V. Figs. 5 and 6). Four specimens were found in the cave of Jerzmanowice.

12. Imperfect specimen of *Cyprœa tigris* (Plate V. Fig. 7). After a thin covering of stalagmite had been removed, the spotted colours of the surface, which had considerably faded, were distinctly to be recognised. This shell, now living in the Indian Ocean, can only have come into the hands of the ancient cave-dwellers by barter. Evidently they must have admired its brilliant spotted exterior.

This unique specimen is from the cave of Sadlana.

c. OBJECTS MADE OF BURNT CLAY.

1. Pieces of pottery were found in nearly every cave at all levels. Those found in the lowest beds are of very rough manufacture, made by the hand alone, but little burnt, and without any glaze. This is more especially the case with the specimen drawn in Plate V. Fig. 12, which is part of a vessel like a pot, with thick sides and of the coarsest workmanship. Large grains of quartz had been mixed with the clay, which is of a dark grey colour, and but little burnt. The substance is so porous, that the vessel can hardly have been used for any fluid.

Other pottery is found evidently of later date and better workmanship, which has been better burnt, but yet is of very rough manufacture. Of this description is the perfect little vessel with a handle, drawn in Plate VI. Fig. 2, found in the cave of Kozarnia.

Some pieces of pottery have impressed ornaments upon them. The ornaments are of various kinds, but on the whole very simple and roughly made. A few of them are drawn (Plate VI. Figs. 3 and 4). Count Zawisza, on his Plates XX. and XXI., has drawn similar specimens from the caves of Wierszchow.

Lastly, some pieces of pottery from the uppermost beds of the floor are evidently of later date, and are consequently of no interest.

2. Spindle whorls of burnt clay; they are of a dark grey or black colour, and of fairly good manufacture (Plate I. Figs. 10–12).

They were found in the caves of Kozarnia, Zbójecka, and Czajowice.

d. OBJECTS MADE OF BRONZE, SILVER, AND IRON.

1. Fibula of bronze (Plate VI. Fig. 6). Only one specimen was found, and that came from the cave of Zbójecka.

2. Bronze ring, ornamented with cross lines; it is not completely closed on one side.[1]

3. Roman silver coin of the age of the Emperors.

The only specimen found was in the cave of Kozarnia, and is drawn (Plate VI. Figs. 7a and 7b). My colleague, Professor Rossbach, has had the kindness to send me the following communication respecting it: 'The coin sent to me is a denarius with the inscription, "Antoninus Augustus Pius P.P. and tribunici: potestat: cons." Probably it may be dated in the year 140. I think in fact that I can see "Consul iterum," Cos. II. But as this is uncertain, the coin being much rusted, and the title of "tribunicia potestas" is not given here, as is frequently the case,

---

[1] This appears to be what is called an armlet or armilla. The shape is exactly the same, the only difference being in the size—those usually found are large enough to be passed over the wrist and 'hammered' tight. This one is much too small for this purpose.—TR.

we cannot positively infer the year 140 to be correct. At all events the only question is as to a year earlier or later. The figure has ears of corn on the right and a cornucopia on the left arm, and consequently is Annona, the goddess of the harvest of field produce, especially of corn.'

As Roman coins have been found in several places in Silesia, probably brought there by traders in amber, whose course led through Silesia to Samland,[1] there does not appear to be anything very striking in the occurrence of this silver coin in the cave of Kozarnia.

4. Iron arrow and lance heads of the usual mediæval form and very much rusted have been found: one of the arrow heads is drawn in Plate VI. Fig. 8.

Lastly, amongst the traces of human activity may be mentioned as an Appendix the occurrence of long bones of the extremities, forcibly broken in order to obtain the marrow. They occur in great numbers in all the caves, frequently associated with charcoal cinders and flint implements. Sometimes the marks of cutting or hammering are distinctly visible upon these bones.

Pieces of stag's horn are also found with decided cut surfaces, evidently intended to be made subsequently into implements.

GENERAL RESULTS.

1. The town of Ojcow is situated about three (German) miles north of Cracow in Russian Poland, and in its immediate neighbourhood. The widely spread white or upper Jura limestone contains numerous caves; the entrances to these caves are in the steep slopes of rocky valleys. In some cases they resemble fissures; in others, they are wider, like a gate or door; they are always from five to ten metres above the level of the valley below, which for the most part is dry. The caves run irregularly several hundred metres into the mountain.

2. The floor of these caves is covered with a deposit, in some cases several metres thick, of dark, brown-grey, tenacious earth, which when moist is plastic and adhesive; this is mixed with angular fragments of limestone, and a few larger blocks of the same stone, which forms the sides of the cavern. Firm beds of coarse crystalline stalagmite are found here and there and at the top.

3. These deposits contain numerous bones of animals and men, and also implements made by human hands.

4. The animal bones belong partly to extinct and partly to recent species. Amongst the

[1] North of Königsberg.—Tr.

latter some are of species now living wild in the neighbourhood of Ojcow; such as the stag, the badger, the fox, the wild cat, &c.; and some are of species now living in the Arctic zone, such as the reindeer, the polar fox, the lemming, &c.

5. By far the greater proportion of the bones belong to the cave bear. A single cave contains the bones of many hundred animals of every age, some of them very young. These numerous cave bears have evidently not lived in the caves at the same period, but are the remains of several succeeding generations for a lengthened period of probably several hundred years.

6. Amongst the other extinct species of animals may be particularly mentioned *Elephas primigenius*, *Rhinoceros tichorhinus* (s. *antiquitatis*), *Hyæna spelæa*, and *Felis spelæa* (Cave Lion), as shown by bones or teeth.

7. The caves have been inhabited by man in different ages, and after very long intervals.

8. The remains of the ancient inhabitants consist of implements of hammered flints (palæolithic, Tr.) and of bone and ivory, altogether excluding all working tools of metal.

9. As teeth and bones of the mammoth (*Elephas primigenius*) were found in the same cave, and apparently in similar beds to those in which the implements of ivory occurred, it appears probable that the ivory implements had been formed of the tusk of a mammoth living contemporaneously with human beings.

10. The co-existence of the cave bear, *Ursus spelæus*, with the oldest human inhabitants of the caves may be proved without a doubt, by the occurrence of a vertebra of this animal, together with a flint implement apparently made by human hands in the same bed of firm crystalline stalagmite.

11. Polished stone implements (neolithic, Tr.) are rare in these caves. As yet only one stone celt of serpentine and another implement of diorite have been discovered.

12. The bronze fibula and rings, found in several of the caves, indicate, both in shape and material, that the inhabitants were at that time of much later date, viz. what is called the 'bronze age.'

13. The human skulls found at a considerable depth below the surface of the floor have been examined by Professor Virchow; there seems to be some little doubt whether they are of the same age as the deposit containing the implements of the most ancient inhabitants. Professor Virchow considers some of the skulls to be dolicho-cephalic, and others to be meso-cephalic. There is, however, no striking peculiarity which indicates any very high antiquity, nor any essential differences in the forms of the skull from those of the present inhabitants of Poland.

FRONTISPIECE.

SKETCH OF A SKULL OF *URSUS SPELÆUS*, FROM THE CAVE OF JERZMANOWICE IN RUSSIAN POLAND.

PLATE I.

FIG.
1. Broad flint knife, one side of which is sharp and the other blunt. Cave of Jerzmanowice.
2. Broad flint implement, notched like a saw at the edge; this serration has evidently been made by hammering. Cave of Jerzmanowice.
3, 4, and 5. Flint knives. Cave of Jerzmanowice.
6. Double-edged flint knife, reduced in size at the bottom. Cave of Jerzmanowice.
7. Double-edged flint knife, pointed at both ends with a median ridge on one side. Cave of Kozarnia.
8. Flint knife. Cave of Zbójecka.
9. Flint knife, elliptical in form, with a median ridge on one side.
10. Spindle whorl of baked clay of dark brown colour. Cave of Jerzmanowice.
11. Spindle whorl of baked clay of dark brown colour. Cave of Czajowice.
12. Spindle whorl of baked clay of dark brown colour. Cave of Kozarnia.

F. Roemer. The Bone Caves of Ojców. Plate I.

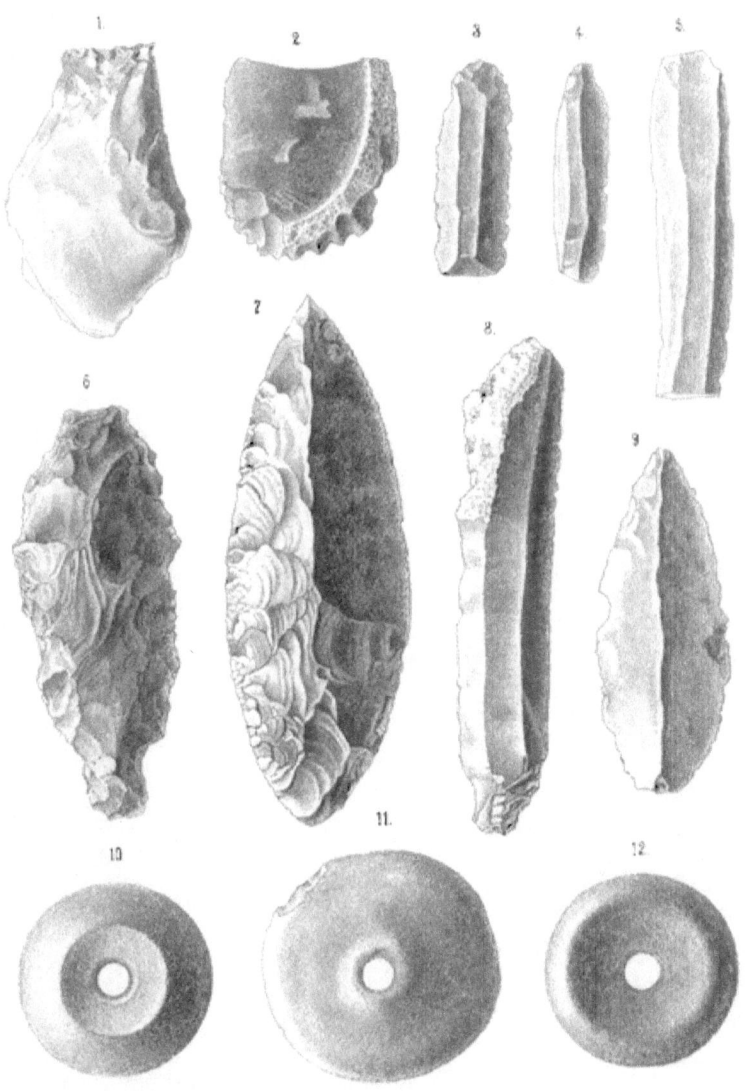

Art. Anst. v. Th. Fischer, Cassel

PLATE II.

FIG.
1. Long flat piece of bone. Use unknown. Cave of Jerzmanowice.
2. Flat ivory rod, compressed at the side, of a lancet shape. From the lower cave of Wierszchow.
3. Perfectly round ivory rod, sharpened at both ends, with a groove round the middle and other ornaments. Use unknown. From the lower cave of Wierszchow.
4. Sharpened bone, forming a boring instrument. Cave of Jerzmanowice.
5. Sharpened bone, forming a boring instrument. Cave of Jerzmanowice.
6. Sharpened bone, forming a boring instrument. Cave of Jerzmanowice.'
7. Sharpened bone, forming a boring instrument, rather larger than the last described, with a circular depression at the larger end, probably the beginning of perforation. Cave of Kozarnia.
8. Sharpened bone, forming a boring instrument. Cave of Jerzmanowice.
9. Sharpened bone, forming a boring instrument. Cave of Sadlana.
10. Small quadrangular bit of bone. Cave of Jerzmanowice.
11. Flat piece of bone, cut off straight on one side. Use unknown. Cave of Zbójecka.
12. Small piece of bone sharpened. Cave of Jerzmanowice.
13. Piece of bone sharpened for a borer, and perforated with a circular hole at the top, which is flat. Cave of Jerzmanowice.

F. Roemer. The Bone Caves of Ojców.   Plate II.

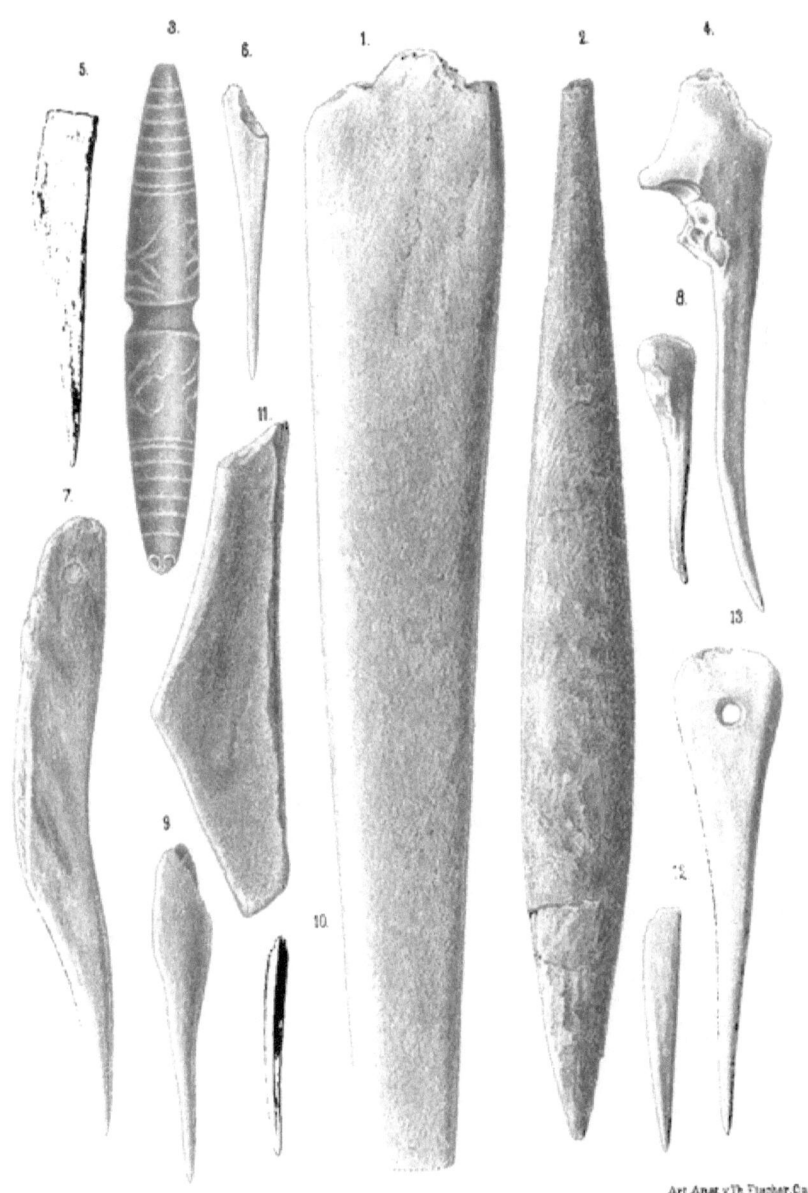

PLATE III.

FIG.
1. Triangular staff of bone, one end of which is cut so as to form a handle. 1 a. Transverse section. Cave of Jerzmanowice.

2. Long bone tool, nearly perfectly circular in section, compressed flat at the upper end, slightly curved.

3. Side view of long bone tool, nearly perfectly circular in section, compressed flat at the upper end, slightly curved. Cave of Jerzmanowice.

4. Elongated bone tool, triangular in section : the three sides are covered with lines scratched in a cross. 4 b. Section of ditto. Cave of Jerzmanowice.

5. Bone tool, nearly perfectly round, compressed at the upper end, and perforated with a round hole. Numerous cross incisions on the surface (surface). Cave of Jerzmanowice.

6. Imperfect bone tool, nearly round, slightly reduced at both ends; the surface here is also covered with cross scratches. Cave of Jerzmanowice.

F. Roemer, The Bone Caves of Ojców. Plate III

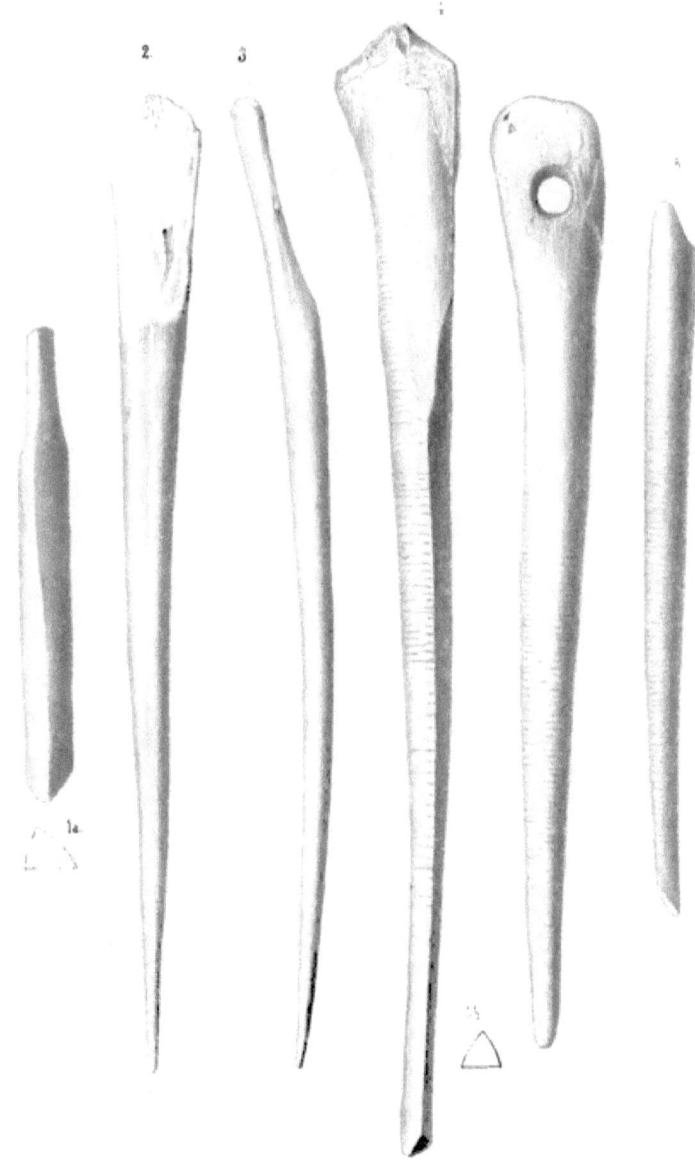

PLATE IV.

FIG.
1. Small rectangular piece of bone, or boar's tusk, perforated with six circular holes. Use unknown. Cave of Sadlana.
2. Boar's tusk ground down flat on one side, and perforated at both ends with a circular hole. Probably worn on a string as an ornament. Cave of Czajowice.
3. Triangular thin plate of bone, perforated with a round hole, evidently made from the os hyoides of a large ruminant. Cave of Sadlana.
4. Small rhomboidal plate of bone perforated in the middle. Cave of Sadlana.
5. Oval piece of ivory, perforated at the narrower end with a large hole. Found by Count Zawisza in the cave of Wierszchow.
6. Irregularly rectangular plate of bone, perforated with two round holes, and also ornamented with seven rows of circular hollows or depressions. Copied from Count Zawisza. Cave of Wierszchow.
7. Canine tooth of cave bear, perforated at the root end with a circular hole; probably worn on a string. Cave of Kozarnia.
8. Boar's tusk, ground down so as to form a curved knife. Cave of Jerzmanowice.
9. Flat implement of stag's horn sharpened at the point and deeply indented below.
10. Bone needle, the upper end with an 'eye,' the lower part broken off.
11. Bone arrow head with a barb, and with the lower part forked. Cave of Jerzmanowice.
12. Implement of the shape of a shovel, sharpened at one end, and made out of the long bone of a large animal. Cave of Jerzmanowice.
13. Straight hollow bird's bone, cut off evenly at one end, and broken at the other. Cave of Zbójecka.
14. A short piece of similar character with cross incisions Cave of Zbójecka.

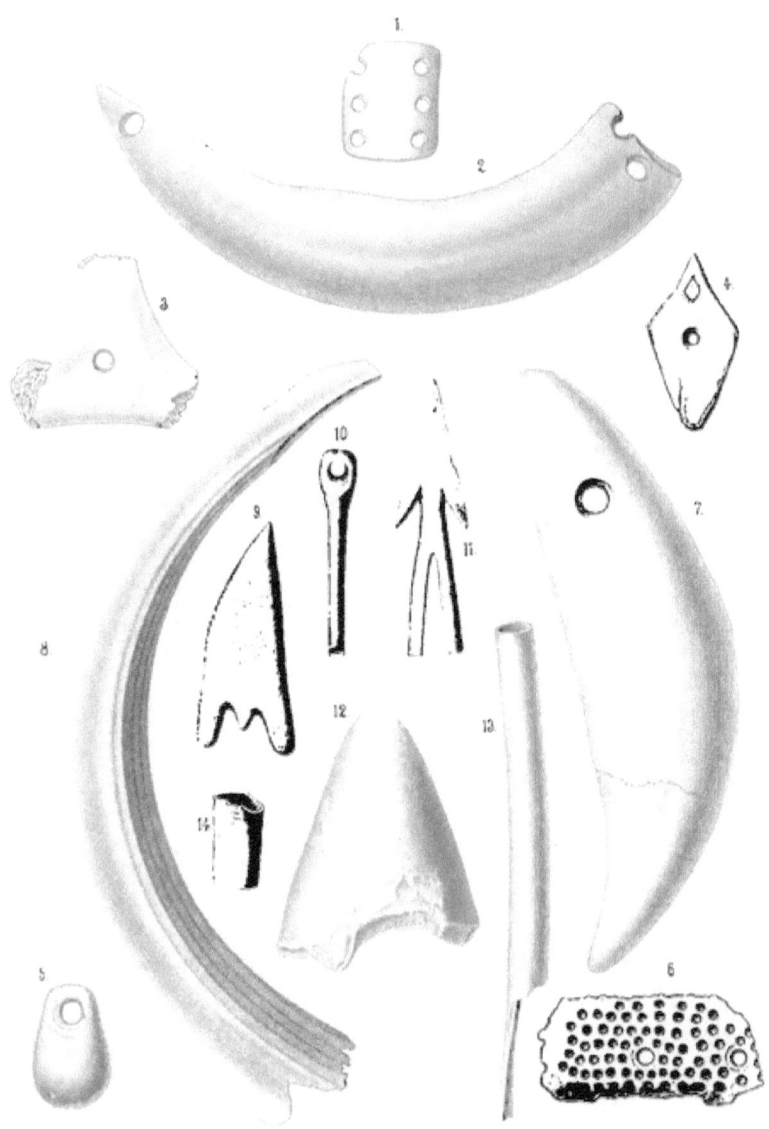

II

PLATE V.

FIG.
1. Brown-red glass bead inlaid with glass threads of a lighter colour; 1a, seen from above; 1b, side view; 1c, the inlaid threads as if seen on a flat surface. See page 37. The inlaid threads have partly weathered away, which may be considered as a proof of high antiquity. Cave of Kozarnia.
2. Dark grey-green glass bead, inlaid with glass threads of a lighter colour; 2a, upper view; 2b, side view; 2c, the ornamentation as if seen on a flat surface. Cave of Kozarnia.
3. Amber bead imperfectly rounded and smoothed; 3a, upper view; 3b, lower and flatter side; 3c, in profile. Cave of Zbójecka.
4. Amber bead; 4a, upper view; 4b, in profile. Cave of Zbójecka.
5. Bone bead; 5a, upper view; 5b, side view. Cave of Jerzmanowice.
6a–6d. Larger beads of bone, irregularly long in shape; viewed in different directions.
7. Imperfect shell of *Cypræa tigris*, from the Indian Ocean; it was partly covered with a thin crust of stalagmite, under which the spotted colouring and pretty polish of the shell can be recognised distinctly. Cave of Sadlana.
8. Polishing stone of black siliceous clay slate. Cave of Kozarnia.
9. Rubbing stone of light coloured sandstone, with furrows and scratches on the surface. Cave of Zbójecka.
10a. Polishing stone of fine-grained sandstone.
10b. Section of polishing stone of fine-grained sandstone.
11. Roundish cuboidal piece of diorite rock, worn down at the sides; evidently has been used for crushing hard bodies (the so-called 'corn crushers'). Cave of Jerzmanowice.
12. Fragment of earthenware vessel, with thick sides, made of burnt clay of very rough manufacture. Cave of Jerzmanowice.

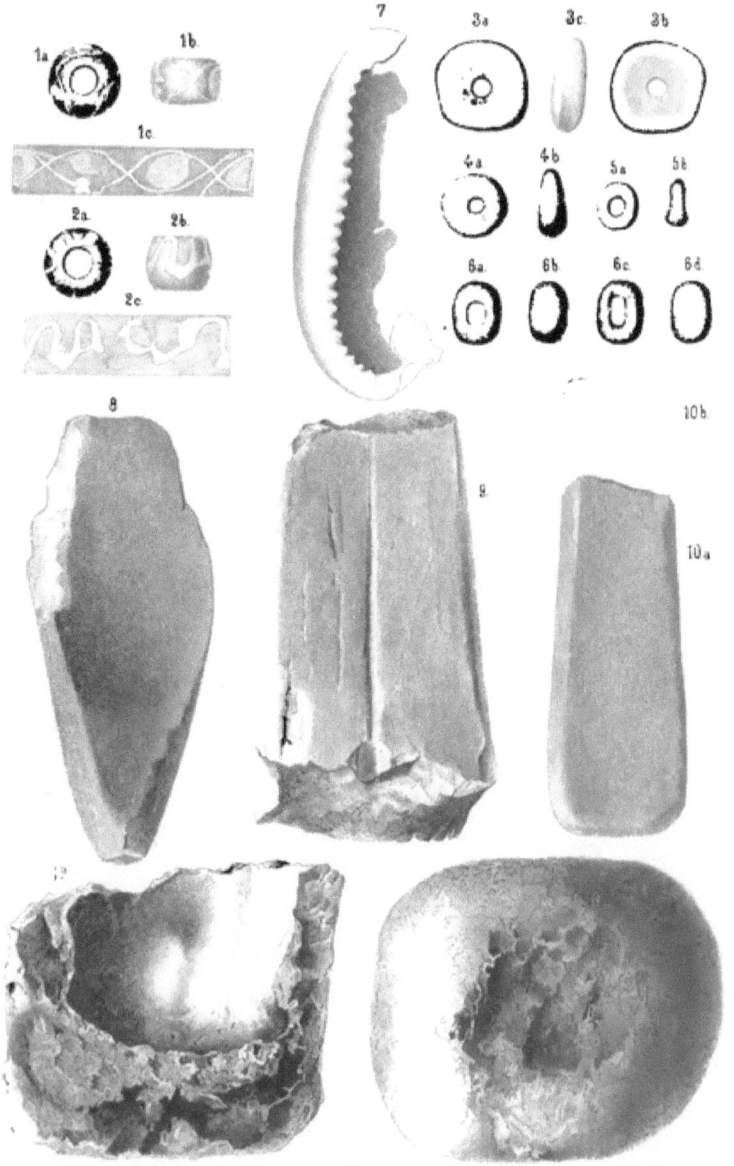

F. Roemer. The Bone Caves of Ojców. Plate V.

PLATE VI.

FIG.

1. A mammalian leg bone, which had been opened by force to get at the marrow. Cave of Zbójecka.

2. Vessel of burnt clay, with a handle, apparently made by the hand alone, imperfectly burnt, and without glaze. Cave of Kozarnia.

3. Pottery roughly ornamented with furrows, and round depressions. Cave of Jerzmanowice.

4. Piece of pottery from the rim of a vessel ornamented with upright parallel impressions, and an impressed set of furrows running round. Cave of Jermanowice.

5. Bronze ring not quite closed in one place (*Armilla?*—Tr.). Cave of Kozarnia.

6. Bronze 'fibula.' Cave of Zbójecka.

7. Roman silver coin. A denarius of the time of Antoninus Pius, probably of the year 140 A.D. 7a shows the side with the head of the Emperor; the other, 7b, has the figure of the goddess Annona, with a cornucopia in her left hand. See page 39. Cave of Kozarnia.

8. Iron lance head very much corroded. Cave of Kozarnia.

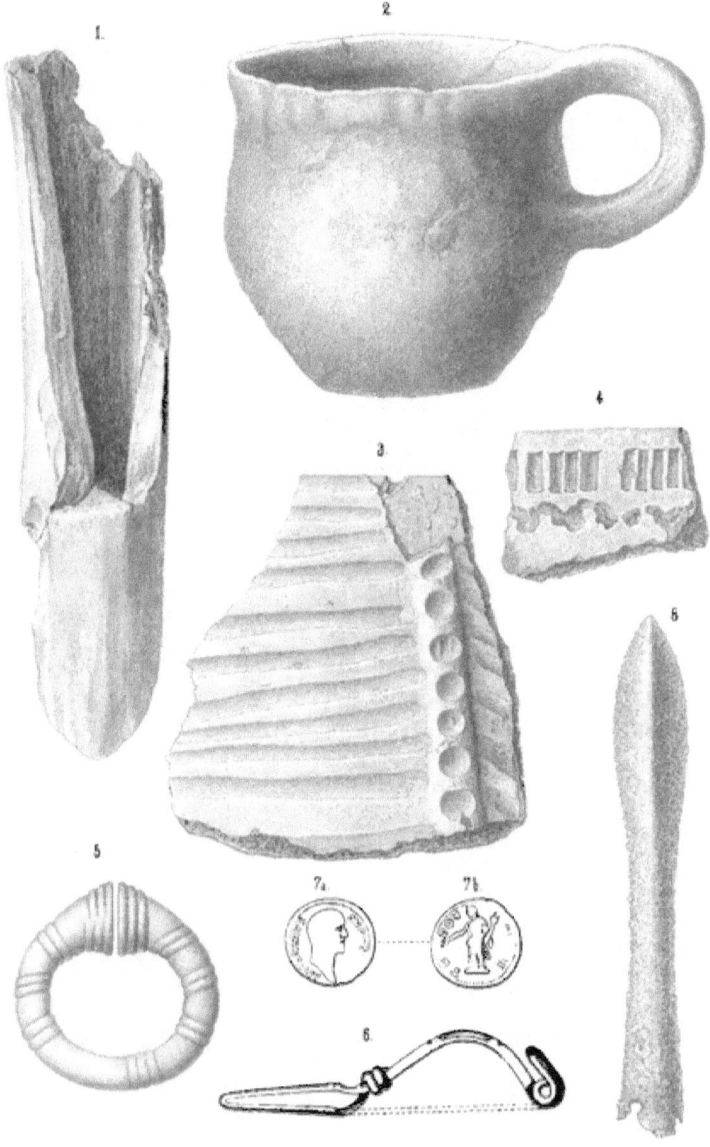

PLATE VII.

FIG.

1. *Ursus spelæus* (Cave Bear).—Canine tooth of the upper jaw; the largest tooth yet found. Cave of Jerzmanowice.

2. *Ursus spelæus* (Cave Bear).—The last molar of the right upper jaw; the largest specimen yet found. Cave of Jerzmanowice.

3. *Ursus spelæus* (Cave Bear).—Os penis. Cave of Jerzmanowice.

4. *Ursus spelæus* (Cave Bear).—Os penis, which had been broken and again healed, but incorrectly joined. A pathological specimen. Cave of Jerzmanowice.

F. Roemer. The Bone Caves of Ojców. Plate VII.

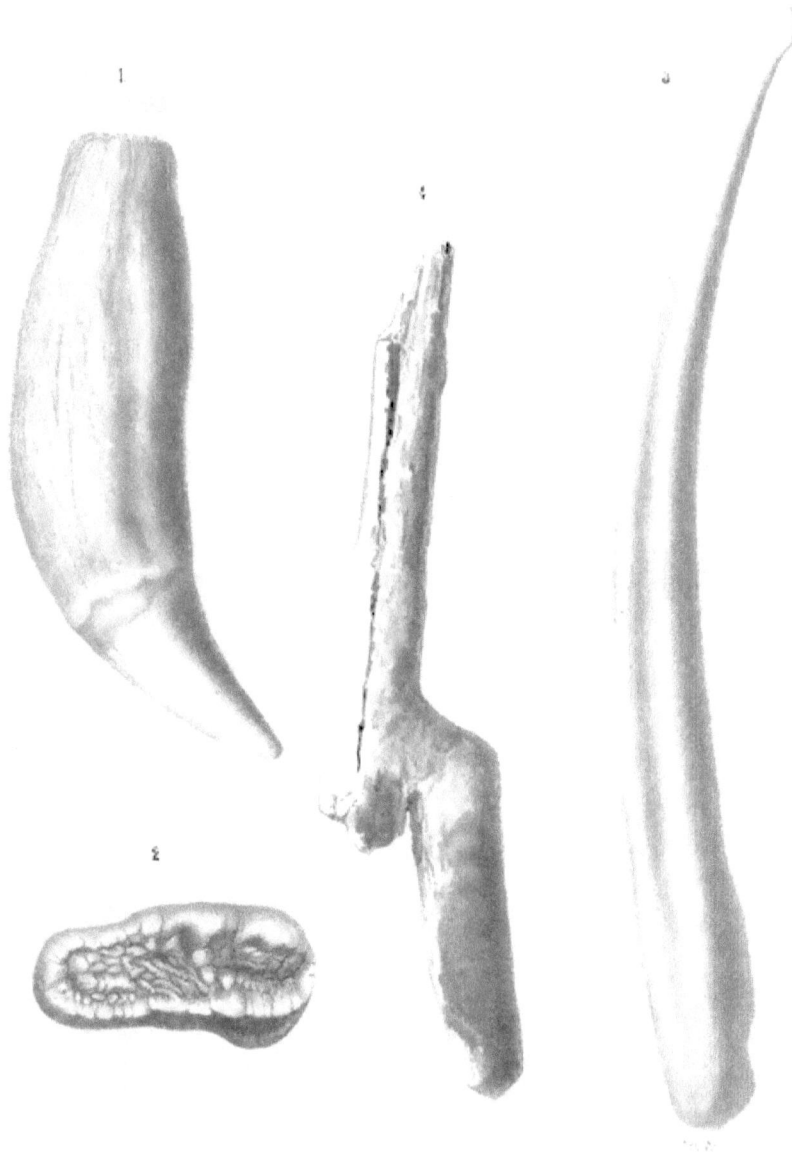

PLATE VIII

FIG.

1. *Felis spelæa* (Cave Lion).—The left under jaw; the canine is wanting. Cave of Jerzmanowice.

1a. *Felis spelæa* (Cave Lion).—Claw of the third toe of the left front foot. The nail sheath has been broken away. Cave of Zbójecka.

2. *Hyæna spelæa* (Cave Hyæna).—Right half of the under jaw, imperfect at the hinder part. Cave of Jerzmanowice.

3. *Felis lynx* (Lynx?).—Left under jaw; the coronoid process is broken off. Cave of Sadlana.

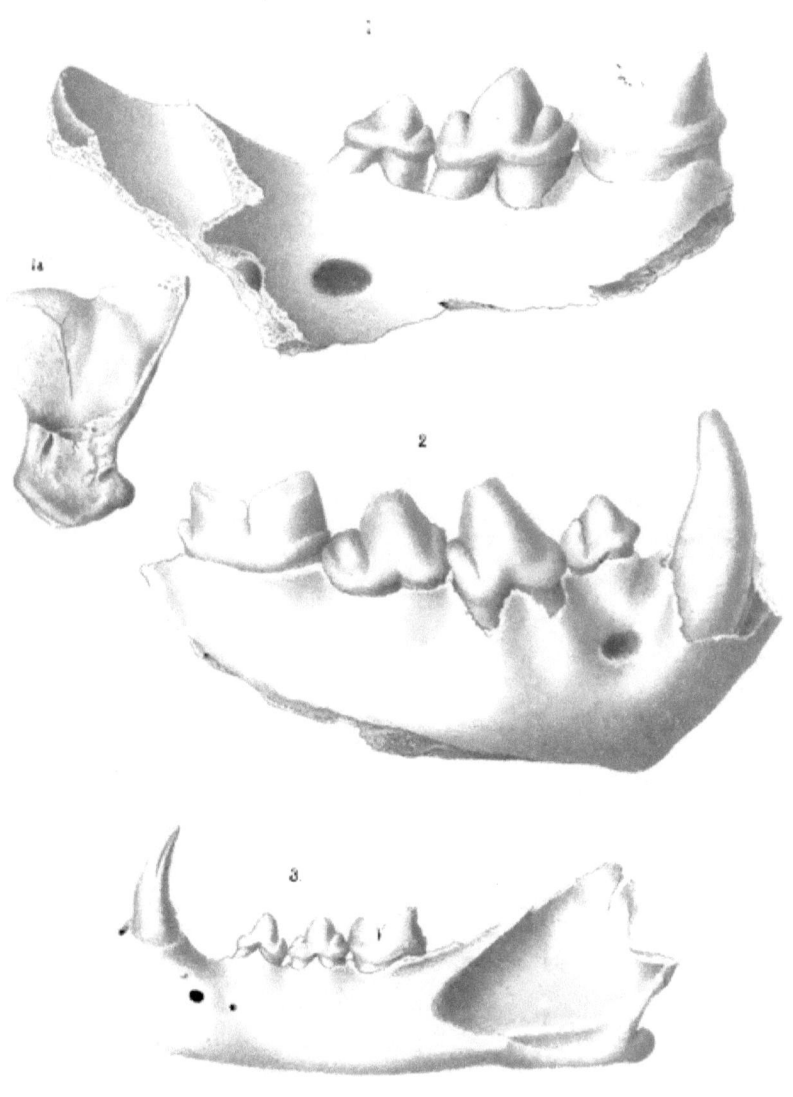

PLATE IX.

FIG.
1. *Canis lupus* (Wolf).—Left under jaw; quite fossil; the canine tooth is wanting. Cave of Zbójecka.

2. *Canis sp.*—This species is in size between the wolf and the fox. The left under jaw. The canine has fallen out. Cave of Kozarnia.

3. *Mustela martes* (Marten).—Right under jaw, quite fossil. Cave of Kozarnia.

4. *Canis lagopus* (Polar Fox).—Left under jaw; the hinder part broken off. Cave of Zbójecka.

F. Roemer. The Bone Caves of Ojcow. Plate IX.

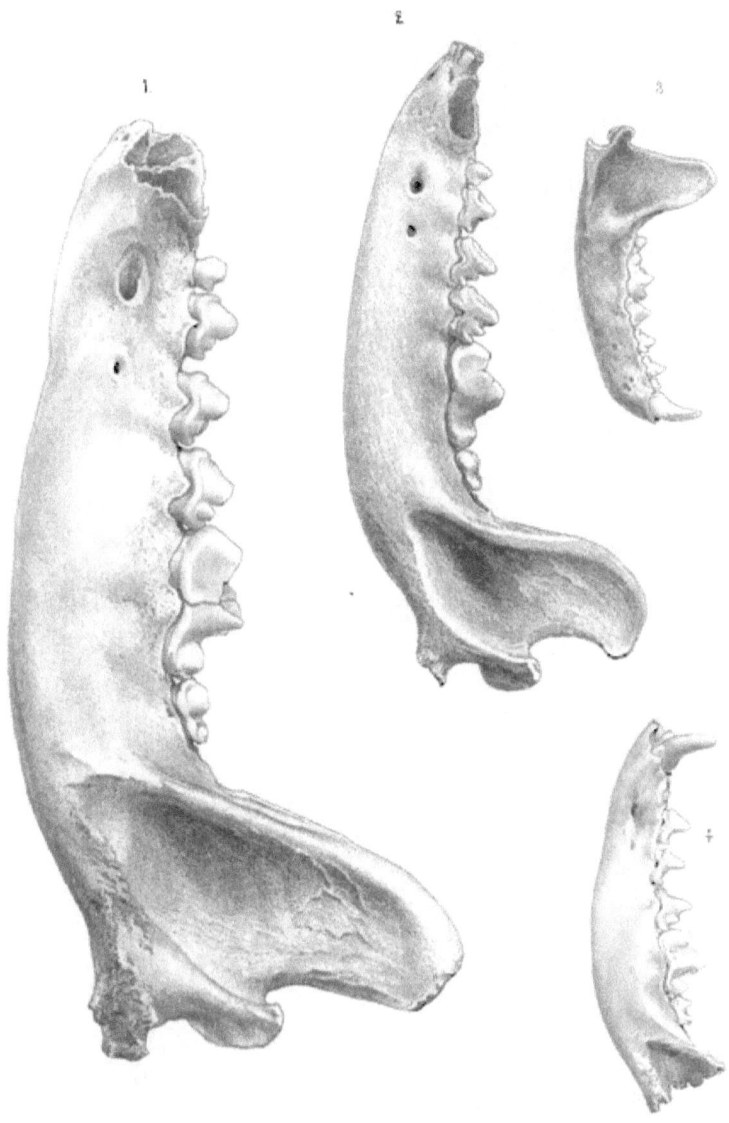

PLATE X.

FIG.

1. *Bos primigenius.*—The last molar of the right under jaw.   Cave of Kozarnia.

2. *Rhinoceros tichorhinus.*—Imperfect molar of the upper jaw.   Cave of Kozarnia.

3. *Elephas primigenius* (Mammoth).—Imperfect end of the tusk of a young animal.   Cave of Zbójecka.

4. *Equus fossilis* (Horse).—A very large terminal phalanx, as seen in front.

4a. *Equus fossilis* (Horse).—Side view of the same.   Cave of Jerzmanowice.

F. Roemer. The Bone Caves of Ojcow. Plate X.

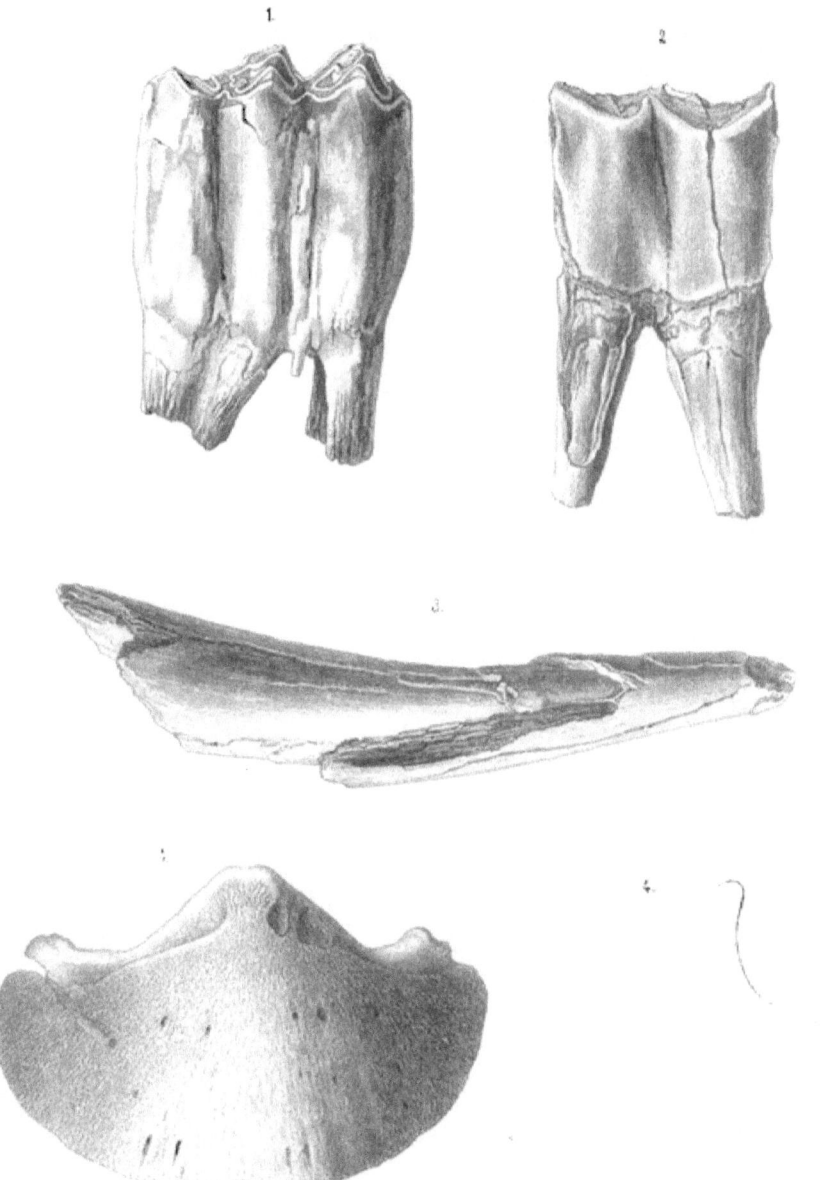

PLATE XI.

FIG.
1. *Bos priscus.*—Left metacarpus. Cave of Jerzmanowice.

2. *Cervus tarandus* (Reindeer).—Part of the antler of a young animal; smooth and even at the lower end, showing that it had been shed naturally.

F. Roemer. The Bone Caves of Ojców.   Plate XI.

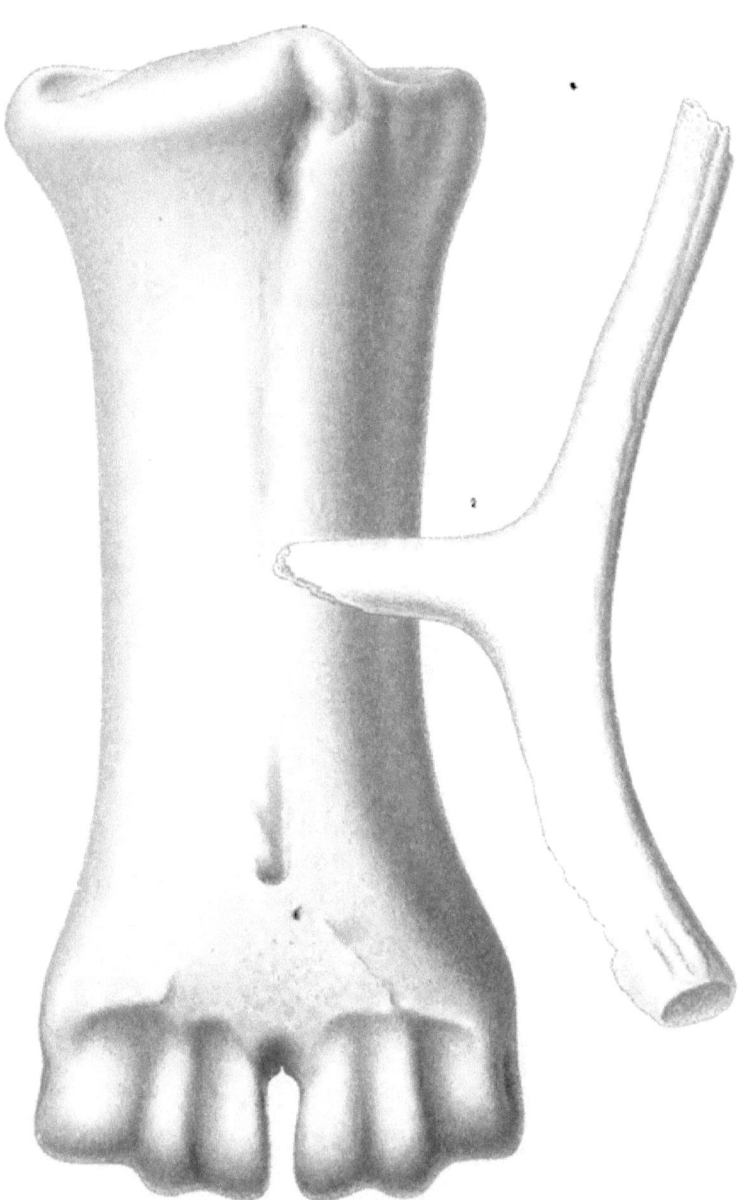

PLATE XII.

FIG.
1. *Cervus tarandus* (Reindeer).—Metatarsus.   Cave of Zbójecka.

2. *Cervus tarandus* (Reindeer).—Imperfect antler of a young animal; the lower part finishes with an even surface, showing that the antler has been naturally shed.

3. *Cervus tarandus* (Reindeer).—Imperfect compressed piece of antler, in the form of a shovel. Both on the surface and within it is porous, and probably it came from a horn not fully grown.   Cave of Górenice.

F. Roemer. The Bone Caves of Ojców. Plate XII.

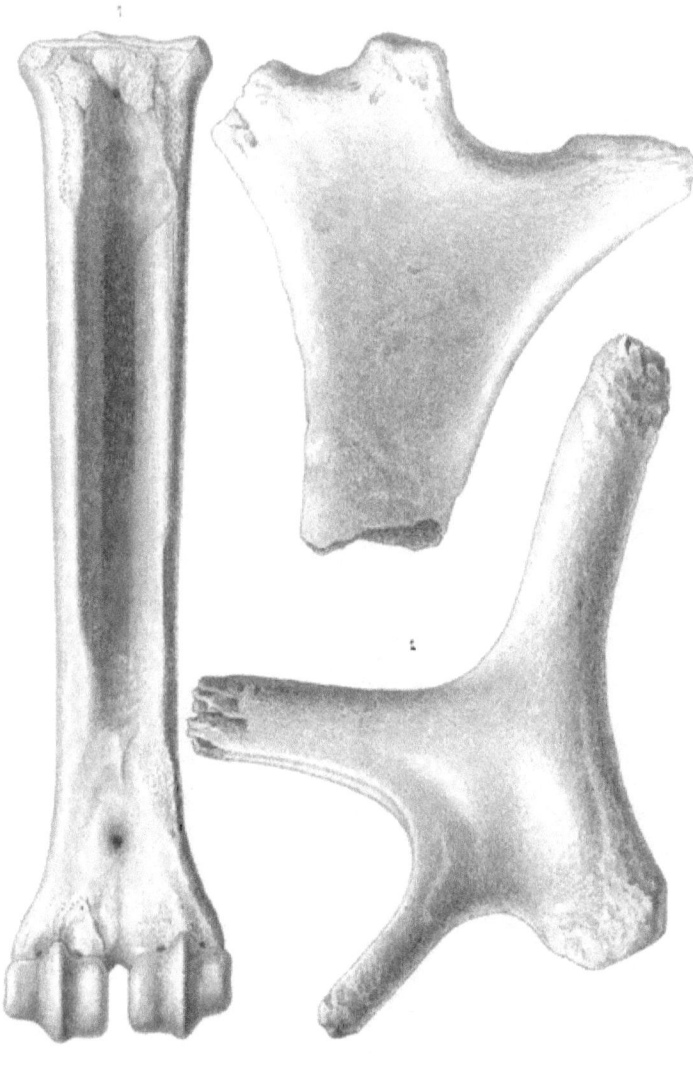

www.ingramcontent.com/pod-product-compliance
Lightning Source LLC
Chambersburg PA
CBHW020158170426
43199CB00010B/1092